THE MARATHON AND HALF MARATHON

THE MARATHON AND HALF MARATHON
A TRAINING GUIDE

Graeme Hilditch

THE CROWOOD PRESS

First published in 2007 by
The Crowood Press Ltd
Ramsbury, Marlborough
Wiltshire SN8 2HR

www.crowood.com

British Library Cataloguing-in-Publication Data
A catalogue record for this book is available from the British Library.

ISBN 978 1 86126 963 8

Disclaimer
Please note that the author and the publisher of this book do not
accept any responsibility whatsoever for any error or omission, nor any
loss, injury, damage, adverse outcome or liability suffered as a result of
the information contained in this book, or reliance upon it. Since the
marathon and the half marathon can be dangerous and could involve
physical activity that is too strenuous for some individuals to engage
in safely, it is essential that a doctor be consulted before undertaking
training.

Photo credits
Great Run/Peter Langdown pages 7, 8, 78, 171; Dartfish page 18;
Polar Electro UK pages 24, 25 (bottom) and 54; Garmin pages 25 (top),
42 and 46; Peter Galbraith (www.fotolia.co.uk) pages 28, 31, 130, 131,
138, 139; London Marathon page 85; Lucozade pages 123 and 124;
Patrick Hermans pages 134, 136.

Edited and typeset by Magenta Publishing Ltd
(www.magentapublishing.com)

Printed and bound in India by Replika Press

Contents

Acknowledgements   6
Introduction   7

1   First Things First   11
2   Welcome to Your Body   27
3   Running Intensity   36
4   Listen to Your Heart   42
5   Stretching and Core Stability   53
6   The Training Part 1: The Importance of Variety   61
7   The Training Part 2: The Half Marathon   77
8   The Training Part 3: The Marathon   85
9   Staying Motivated   93
10 Nutrition For Running   96
11 Fluids: Balancing Fluids For Performance   119
12 Running Injuries: Their Diagnosis and Treatment   129
13 Special Precautions for Older and Female Runners   143
14 Race Day   150

Further Information   173
Index   175

Acknowledgements

To my forever-patient wife Jo, who has persevered with late nights and my fluctuating moods whilst I have been writing this book.

To Simon Thornley, for the kind loan of photographic equipment and his invaluable advice on sports photography.

To Wigs Cato and Zahra Severn for their time and invaluable help with the photographic element of the book. Without their help, none of the included images would have been possible.

The Cotswold Leisure Centre, for their cooperation in the use of their gym and facilities for a selection of images.

To Dartfish, Lucozade, Polar and Garmin for kindly providing imagery.

To the Bath and Bristol half marathon, the Great North Run and the London Marathon for their assistance with imagery and statistics.

And finally to my parents Lynn and Cliff, for their support and encouragement throughout my professional career.

Introduction

For many people, the mere thought of subjecting their mind, soul and cherished body to a 13.1 mile (21 kilometre) or 26.2 mile (42.1 kilometre) run, is enough to make them feel exhausted – and to be frank who can blame them?

For most of us, a full-time career and twenty-four hour family commitments make the sofa and TV remote control a pair of luxury items we would happily pay to spend more time with. To contemplate sacrificing this indulgence for a tracksuit, trainers and the open road seems nothing short of crazy.

Curiosity, however, eventually gets the better of thousands of people every year. Once in a while during those precious minutes in front of the TV, a closet marathon wannabe will inadvertently tune into live coverage of a famous half or full marathon. It is then, if only for a short time, that the curiosity sets in. The sight of tens of thousands of men and women from every walk of life, all helping to raise millions for charity, subtly embeds itself into the mind and the question is quietly raised – 'Could I do that?'

The mixed emotions of finishing an endurance race.

Did You Know...

- During a marathon you will burn approximately 2,500 calories – as many as an average man should consume per day.
- In 1981 there were 7,747 applicants for the London Marathon; this increased to 46,500 in 2003.
- There are in excess of 800 organized marathons in the world every year – 384 in the USA alone.
- The fastest half marathon, at time of print, was run by Haile Gebrselassie of Ethiopia, who finished the Phoenix Half Marathon in Arizona in a time of 58 minutes 55 seconds. That is a pace of around 4:30 minutes/mile.
- The fastest marathon, at time of print, was run by Paul Tergat of Kenya, who completed the Berlin Marathon in a time of 2 hours, 4 minutes, 55 seconds. That is an average pace of around 4:46 minutes/mile (12.6 miles per hour/20.3 kilometres per hour).
- If you are worried about running the slowest ever marathon, don't panic. The slowest time for the event was recorded by Lloyd Scott, who crossed the finishing line in a time of 5 days, 8 hours, 29 minutes and 46 seconds. He did have a half-decent excuse, though – he competed in the race wearing a 130lb (59kg) diver's suit.

As much as people try to shake off the ridiculous proposition of running a marathon, once the seed is planted it simply refuses to go away. Eventually, the question of 'Could I do that?' changes to 'I could do that!'

The radical change of heart, from throw-away comments aimed at the TV of 'Those people are nuts' to 'I reckon I could do that' may take weeks, months or years; however long it has taken, the fact that you are reading this book shows it has happened to you.

The popularity of long-distance running events has increased dramatically over the past twenty years. The number of people taking part in the London Marathon since the early 1980s has increased by an amazing 500 per cent.

Running in a half or full marathon is an experience you will never forget, and it will earn you bragging rights for years to come. Whether you compete as a vegetable, a super-hero or yourself, you will not only be raising valuable money for charity but you will go through a number of uplifting emotions both in your training and in the race itself that you will always remember. The whole experience will instil numerous emotions that will make you laugh and cry, but one thing is for sure – you will never regret doing it.

A poignant sight, typical at marathons.

The elation of crossing the line.

Unfortunately, you can't turn up at the start line without having put some miles in those legs. In the months leading up to the race you will need to adapt your body to endure the demands of running a distance you may never have imagined possible. You will have the joy of running in beautiful sunshine, horizontal rain and maybe even snow but the training can be hugely enjoyable and give you a real sense of achievement.

This book is a step-by-step guide covering all aspects of your training, for both the full and the half marathon. From the running itself, to nutrition and the injuries you may experience, this book will help you every step of the way, guiding you through your first training run right through to the elation of crossing the finishing line.

Before you jump straight to the training programmes in chapters 7 and 8, I would strongly advise you to read through all of the chapters that explain the training processes. The training programmes are certainly useful to follow and offer a very good guide as to the mileage you should be covering every week, but devising a training plan to suit everyone is an impossible task – despite my best efforts. Everyone will have different circumstances and times available to train, so following any of the plans to the letter could either be too easy or far too difficult. It is for this very reason that you must develop an understanding of the adaptation processes involved, before you can attempt to start training. Once you understand why each session should be performed at a certain pace or length of time, you are then strongly placed to effectively rewrite the three/four month training plan to suit your individual circumstances and ability.

HOW TO USE THIS BOOK

All runners, irrespective of ability, have varying levels of interest in the way the running body

You are an individual – train like one.

works. A quick runner may have little desire to learn how and why the body responds to certain training methods, just as a slow runner may strive to learn everything there is to know about the adaptation process of endurance training. I personally believe that if you are undertaking an endurance training regime, and with it the huge demands placed on your body, a sound knowledge of running physiology is essential.

By understanding why certain training methods are used and how they affect your body, you are in a far better position to know if your training is effective or if you are under- or overdoing it.

Ultimately, the level of understanding you wish to acquire is up to you. With this in mind, this book is laid out in such a way that you can skip over chapters that are of no interest to you, and concentrate on the areas that you find more useful. The depth this book goes into is more than sufficient for the majority of those competing in half and full marathons. It does not go into excessive depth worthy of a Ph.D. in exercise science, for the simple reason that information overload invariably over-complicates matters and confuses people unnecessarily.

If you do wish to gain a greater understanding of any of the topics covered in this book, and wish to significantly improve your performance to be able run a very fast race, I strongly advise runners to seek further reading material. However, a word of caution. You will find that the more you read, the more contradiction you will discover in various training theories. This can be confusing, leaving you with no clear idea as to who is right and who wrong. The best advice I can offer is that you approach all material you read with an open mind, and decide which theory suits your unique individuality. You are an individual – train like one.

CHAPTER 1

First Things First

GET A CHECK-UP

In the 2005 Flora London Marathon a fit man of 28 crossed the finishing line in just over four hours. He tragically died three hours later, after suffering a brain haemorrhage. He was taken ill after the race and passed away whilst on the way to hospital. For weeks he had been complaining of headaches after his training sessions, but shrugged off the symptoms as tiredness and dehydration. It is possible that, had he had a medical check-up, his symptoms would have been picked up by his GP and treatment could have saved his life.

Events like this are of course rare, but they do happen every year. Although it may be an obvious statement to include in any training guide, it is advisable to visit your GP and have a check-up before you begin training. It may

seem like an unnecessary precaution, especially if you are not new to running, but the death of this fit young athlete illustrates that problems can occur during endurance events. Even the most minor of symptoms is worth getting checked out.

Although a check-up by your GP may not uncover all underlying health problems, it will certainly put your mind at rest that he/she is happy for you to begin a training regime. It is also worth mentioning to your doctor if any of your family members have died or suffered ill health from any form of cardiac illness.

WE ARE UNIQUE

During my career as a personal trainer, I have trained many people for both the marathon and half marathon, all with varied running ability and experience. Along with blisters,

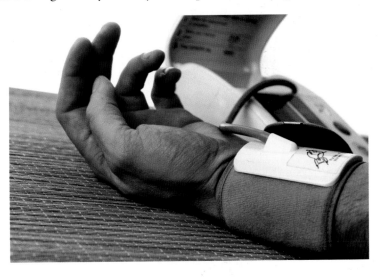

Get a medical check-up before you begin training.

Examples of Individuality

- The amount of blood ejected from the heart per minute varies from 6.7 pints (3.16 litres) to a massive 22.8 pints (10.81 litres).
- The amount of air passed in and out of the lungs per breath per minute varies from 7.4 pints (3.5 litres) to 30.4 pints (14.4 litres).
- The number of times the heart beats every minute at rest can vary from 45 beats to 105 beats.

---

muscle niggles and the occasional expletive, all the runners have one thing in common. Every person I have trained for an endurance event has, at one time or another, posed a question like 'My friend who has run loads of marathons told me that there was no need for this type of training', or 'I read in a magazine that what you are telling me is wrong.'

Although every question is different, often I have very little room for argument; not through lack of knowledge but simply because endurance training is not an exact science. Certain physiological principles are the same for all of us, such as that running too fast too soon will lead to premature fatigue, and a low supply of carbohydrate will greatly hinde performance, but when it comes to trainin everyone is different. Due to our individu ality, it is nearly impossible to apply a 'on rule fits all' philosophy to running practice nutrition or even injury.

Every year runners are bombarded wit statements like 'You only need to do one lon run before the race' and 'These are the bes trainers for marathons.' This causes som to completely change their training sched ules halfway through, all because a frien suggested doing it differently.

The importance of training and eating t meet your own individual requirements is point that will be reiterated throughout thi book, and used as a constant reminder tha just because someone else is running 10 miles a week or eating 4lb of pasta a day, i doesn't necessarily mean you should too You can read all the running and nutritio guides in the world, but to run well yo need to listen to your body and do wha suits you!

Throughout the book, all the major nutri tional and training processes that your bod will encounter throughout your preparatio

Two runners, each with unique abilities.

Choose your event – 13.1 or 26.2 miles?

will be explained. In the following chapters you will learn how your body is able to adapt to withstanding over three hours of running, how energy is supplied to fuel your training and what may cause your performance to deteriorate. So, even if you decide to seek additional advice, this book will provide you with the knowledge to decide if it is advice worth following.

WHICH EVENT?

At this stage, you may or may not know which race you want to train for. For some people, the idea of training for the full 26.2 miles is too daunting; for others it offers the ultimate challenge. Many people new to running first decide (sensibly) to see how they get on with the half marathon and then make the decision whether to go for the full distance.

Whichever event you choose it is important that you enjoy the training and, above all, enjoy the experience. There are plenty of opportunities to compete in other races, so do not feel pressured to push yourself unnecessarily.

If you have a particular event in mind, make sure you are aware of the conditions that you will be training in. For example, the Flora London Marathon is always in April,

and therefore the majority of the training will need to be done in the British winter. This may be ideal for some runners as it is extremely unlikely, despite global warming, that any long training runs will take place in oppressive heat. However, on the other side of the coin the prospect of training in snow blizzards, 50mph gales and in light that vanishes at 4pm can be a little difficult to come to terms with. These factors should not put you off, but it is important that you think about which conditions and therefore which event is going to suit you the best.

A number of websites listed on page 173 offer great advice and details of events in and around your locality. Information such as course profile, quality of organization and facilities as well as the number of runners is explained, so you can make your own mind up as to which race you'd like to run in.

CHOOSE A CHARITY

Depending on the event you decide to enter, securing a place can be very difficult. The London Marathon, New York Marathon and the Great North Run are just some examples where the demand for places is so great that many people are disappointed. In

*Two runners
supporting
each other.*

these cases, the only way to guarantee admission is through one of the many charities that purchase places through the event organizers. The number of places each charity has to offer generally depends on the size of the individual charity but they vary from half a dozen to several hundred.

Most people have a charity that they feel strongly about, so to make the hard work more worthwhile it is best if you approach your favourite and enquire about a place for the event you are interested in. In return for guaranteed entry, you effectively commit yourself to raise a certain amount of money set by the charity. This amount is usually in the region of £1,500 for marathons and slightly less for half marathons. All charities give you a generous amount of time to raise the funds, so there is no need to panic about letting your charity down.

For the lucky few, the larger events such as London and New York offer a number of places via a ballot. You can apply for these ballot places by registering with the organizers, and then all you can do is hope for the best. If you are lucky enough to be selected,

you are guaranteed entry and are not required to raise any money for charity – an option most ballot runners do not opt for. Running in an endurance event provides you with the perfect opportunity to raise valuable funds for charity. You will be pleasantly surprised with the generosity of family, friends and strangers when you ask for sponsorship. Everyone is aware of the commitment and effort you are putting into your training, so most people are happy to donate money to the cause.

For the smaller, less popular events entry is easier. Generally, the format is that you pay an admission fee and are offered a place. As with ballot places, there is no specific requirement for you to raise any money for charity but it is certainly worthwhile asking friends and family for a contribution.

EMOTIONAL SUPPORT

During the months of training ahead, you will experience a rollercoaster of emotions. From your first 'runner's high', to the fatigued legs after your first run of over an hour, there are times when you will reflect on what you

OPPOSITE: *A charity runner enjoying her big day.*

are doing and feel a huge sense of self-pride, and other times when you are exhausted and desperately want to quit.

It is at times like this when you will need the support of the people closest to you. Although the low points may not happen very often, it is a good idea to give your nearest and dearest prior warning that you will need their support and encouragement.

Runners' forums on the Internet provide a means of support and consolation with fellow runners, and can be an excellent way t offload your worries and negative thought onto others who are invariably feeling th same way, especially if they are training for th same event. Family and friends are fantasti for moral support, but communicating wit other runners who are experiencing what yo are going through can make you feel so muc better. It is reassuring to know that you ar not the only one who feels despondent from time to time.

The correct running apparel is essential.

Good quality trainers are worth every penny.

WHAT TO WEAR

Thankfully, the dress sense of runners has drastically improved over recent years. If you wear luminous headbands and garish tracksuit bottoms for a race you are now more likely to be classed as a fancy dress runner rather than a serious athlete.

Irrespective of vanity, the most important factor in determining your running attire is comfort. The manufacturing of sports clothing has advanced hugely in recent years, making clothes more breathable and slimline, but ultimately if you are not comfortable in them they could hamper your preparations.

The following guidelines tell you what to look for in clothing and the considerations you should make, depending on your circumstances.

Running Shoes

Your running shoes are without doubt the most important item of clothing you will buy as part of your running kit.

You cannot afford to go for the cheap option, as cheap trainers are unlikely to have the durability to withstand your demanding running schedule. You should be looking to spend anything upwards of £60 ($100) for a decent pair of running shoes and it is likely that you will need two pairs to see you up to race day. They must be comfortable, mould to your feet well and above all be the right type of shoe for your 'running gait' (overleaf).

Trousers and Shorts

Depending on the climate that you are running in, you are going to need to buy a quality pair of running trousers and/or shorts. In the early stages of your training, the type of trousers or shorts you wear will make no apparent difference to the comfort of your run, but as distances increase the difference becomes very noticeable.

When buying running trousers look for known brands such as Nike, Adidas, Ron Hill and Asics who manufacture specialized trousers to help minimize drag, wick sweat away from the legs and reduce the chances of chafing in embarrassing places. Normal tracksuit bottoms may be fine for a short jog, but for runs of any noticeable distance they become very uncomfortable and you will only end up wishing that you had spent that little bit more on a decent pair of trousers.

In warmer weather, shorts will help to keep you cool and prevent you from overheating. The leading manufactures are once again the ideal choice as they produce shorts that are not only lightweight but also help to 'air' areas of your midriff to keep you comfortable throughout your workout.

Whichever item you decide to wear come race day, it is important that you wear your trousers or shorts a number of times before

Running Gait

The term running gait is one that new and experienced runners are becoming more familiar with, and they are beginning to realize how important it is to choose trainers that best match the way they run. Incorrect shoes for your gait can lead to a number of injuries, from ankle pain to hip pain. These injuries are discussed in more detail in Chapter 12.

Your running gait, put simply, is the way in which you run. Imagine the way a car is set up; if it is set up incorrectly or out of kilter, the tyres (your trainers) can wear unevenly and place stress on the axle (your legs). By choosing the right shoes, you can redress the imbalance and greatly reduce the risk of contracting a biomechanical injury.

Running Gait Assessment

Having your running gait assessed before you begin training is essential. With the help of specialized computer software and running gait specialists, your running pattern can be analysed and accurate advice can be offered as to which type of shoe you should choose. This procedure may seem like an expensive and inaccessible luxury, but you would be wrong on both counts. This service is usually free and leaves you with peace of mind, knowing that the shoes you use for your training are the right ones.

There are a number of running assessment systems available, some of which travel nationwide, making them easily accessible for runners all over the country. The assessment procedure is carried out by using a pressure pad or a treadmill. The athlete runs on the pad/treadmill and the operator can see where the foot impact is heaviest and how your feet land when you run. From this analysis, you will be advised with a great deal of accuracy if you are an 'over-pronator', 'neutral' or an 'under-pronator'.

A running gait analysis using video technology.

Over-pronators

Asics, the trainer manufacturer, claim that around 70 per cent of runners over-pronate. Over-pronators tend to land on the very outer edge of the heel and as the foot progresses through the movement it rolls inwards, causing the inner forefoot to take excessive pressure. This places a larger amount of stress on the inside of the foot through the mid-stance and propulsion stage of the running movement. Over a short period of time this poses no problem to the runner, who is likely to be unaware of any present or potential injury. However, over time this imbalance causes certain muscles to over-work, leading to pain and inflammation in the ankles, shins, knees and hips.

Although gait analysis can easily identify over-pronators, there is a less technical way to see if you are an over-pronator. Simply take a look at a pair of sports shoes you have used for several months. If you notice excessive wear on the rear outer edge of your shoe and a significant indent on the insole where your big toe goes it is likely that you over-pronate. Although you will not be able to change the way you run, potential injury caused by over-pronating can be avoided by ensuring you have the correct shoes.

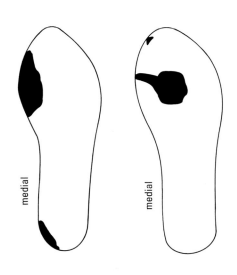

Severe over-pronation.　　*Moderate over-pronation*

Neutral Runners

Oh, what it is to be perfect. Neutral runners, as the name suggests, run with a neutral gait, which is regarded as the ideal running motion. Right through from the heel strike to foot propulsion, the foot maintains a balanced transition through the stride, placing no undue stress on the lower leg muscles.

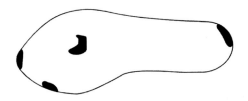

Neutral.

Under-pronators

Runners who under-pronate are rare. The gait cycle takes the foot from heel strike to propulsion on the outside of the foot. Under-pronation, like over-pronation, can cause a number of injuries that could severely hamper your training.

It is important that you get your stride analysed as soon as you can, so that if you need special shoe inserts (known as orthotics and prescribed by a podiatrist) to rebalance your running stride, you can use them right at the beginning of your training and greatly reduce your chances of contracting an injury. Don't be a statistic – get yourself checked out and analysed.

continued overleaf

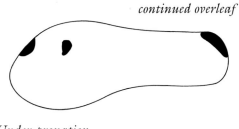

Under-pronation.

Running Gait *continued*

Soggy Foot Test

Before you get your feet and stride profession-ally analysed, why not have a look for yourself to see what kind of feet you have. The purpose of the soggy foot test is to find out the structure of the soles of your feet. Depending on what you see, it can be a preliminary indicator of what type runner you are – over-pronator, neutral or under-pronator.

All you need to do is wet one of your feet and walk on a surface that will show you an imprint – a piece of brown paper or even a tiled bathroom floor is ideal. The imprint left will tell you one of three things – whether you have sunken or low arches, neutral arches or high arches.

Low arches indicate that you are likely to be an over-pronator, as there is little support to stop your food rolling inwards. Neutral arches indicate that your feet are ideal for running and high arches indicate that you could be an under-pronator.

The final point to make about trainers is that it is vital that you do not decide to compete in the race with a new pair of running shoes. New trainers usually cause a little rubbing on the first few runs as they take time to mould to your feet, so don't be alarmed if you get a blister or two. Every year, people turn up at the start line with a new, dazzling pair of shoes. They may win a prize for best-dressed runner, but come mile 18 when the blisters on your feet grow to the size of small water balloons, the accolade no longer seems so attractive!

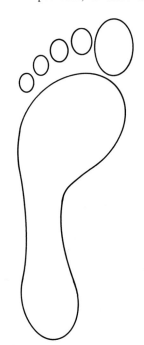

Neutral foot imprint.

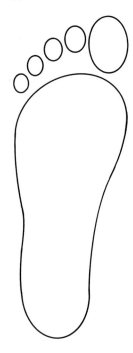

Dropped arches – likely to be an over-pronator.

Raised arches – likely to be an under-pronator.

Lightweight shorts or trousers are vital.

to ensure that they fit properly and do not chafe certain areas. As amusing as the term 'chafing' may sound, it really can cause significant discomfort on a run. Many runners apply petroleum jelly to commonly affected areas just before the race.

Briefs

What you decide to wear under your trousers or shorts is up to you. Cycling shorts, suitable underwear and jockstraps are all used but ultimately the choice is yours. Some runners wear nothing under their trousers, others opt for just cycling shorts and do away with trousers altogether. There is no right answer, so wear something that is not going to rub. Experiment to find out what suits you.

Tops

The type of top you wear must reflect the climate that you are running in as heat has a major effect on your running performance. The harder your body has to work to keep you cool, the more energy you will expend, causing premature fatigue. It is essential that you wear the right top for your training as well as the race itself.

The most important features of a top are that it does not rub and is breathable. If the weather is cold when you start out then it is fine to wear another lightweight top as well; just tie it around your waist when you warm up. On race day, if the weather is cold, most runners wear old tops that they don't mind throwing away at the start of the race. This saves the hassle of tying it around your waist.

On warmer days, a singlet or vest are the most appropriate tops but once again watch out for rubbing. Some running vests are cut fairly high under the arm, which can cause underarm soreness over a long run. Just make sure that, come race day, your running gear has been tried and tested on training runs.

Buy quality tops, to avoid chafing.

Socks

Despite their being the smallest item o clothing, buying the correct socks is very important. The amount of sweat your fee produce during exercise is probably a lo more than you think. If you wear cheap socks that do not wick sweat away from th

skin and do not allow your feet to breathe, the salt and the moisture in your sweat soon lead to blisters. It is advisable to spend that little bit more on a few pairs of specialized running socks to give yourself the best chance of avoiding blisters.

Peripherals

Reflective Strips
If you plan to train in the dark or in poor light, it is essential that you wear a reflective top or strip so that you are clearly visible to oncoming vehicles. Even if you feel you can dodge oncoming traffic, drivers can easily be startled by suddenly noticing a runner in their path, potentially causing an accident. Reflective tape and vests can be bought cheaply from a number of outlets.

Water Bottles and Belt
During your shorter training runs there is no real need to take on fluids, but as the distances you run increase it is important that you drink to prevent dehydration. To ease the burden of carrying a large, cylindrical-shaped water bottle on long runs, runner-friendly water bottles are available with a hole in the middle, making fluid a lot easier to carry. If you prefer, water belts are also available so that you can place the bottle in a special waist strap.

Ideally, strategically placing water bottles on the route where you run is the best option, but this is not always possible or practical in built-up areas. Ultimately, the choice is yours but try to make the process of re-hydration during your training as easy as possible.

Mp3 Player
With modern audio technology getting smaller by the year, Mp3 players are the perfect runner's companion. As light as a feather and able to hold more songs than five back-to-back marathons, Mp3s offer an escape from the sound of your pounding feet. Running to your favourite music can

Music and fluid – an endurance runner's best friends.

be incredibly uplifting and some reports suggest that it can even improve your exercise performance. Obvious care must be taken when running near traffic but if you are worried about a two-hour jog becoming mundane, an Mp3 player may be able to help you out.

Hats and Gloves
Once again, the weather is a determining factor in the use of a hat and gloves. As you warm up, the blood in your body is redistributed to the working muscles of your legs. This leaves the extremities, such as your hands, with a reduced volume of blood, making them that much more sensitive to the cold. Some people suffer from this more than others, so the choice and necessity of hats and gloves is an individual one.

Use technology to help your training.

Running Gadgets

The size of your wallet determines not only how high-tech your tops and bottoms are but also the type of accessories you choose to train with. Buying gadgets such as GPS systems, inertial distance measuring pods, Mp3 players, pedometers and heart rate monitors will certainly make your credit card company happy but it's up to you what kind of gadgetry you use.

Although in principle all you need to run are trainers and clothes, I would recommend investing in one or two of the following items. They needn't cost the earth but they will make your training more effective, safer and a little more interesting.

Distance Measuring Devices

Knowing the distances you are covering is an important part of training. Although it can be argued that the time it takes you to do a run is equally beneficial, I believe if you are to be competing in a 13.1 mile or 26.2 mile race it gives you peace of mind knowing how far you are able to run at every stage of your training.

There are a number of ways to determine how far you are running, with no one way being better than the other. The determining factor is based on where you do the majority of your running. Using a car to measure a certain route is a very accurate way of determining distance, but for those who train on country paths this may not be a practical idea. In cases such as this, distance measuring devices are invaluable. The three most popular are pedometers, GPS and inertial technology.

Pedometers Pedometers are by far the cheapest alternative. They are placed unobtrusively on your running trousers and work by measuring the number of steps you take and multiplying it by your stride length, which you input before your run. As soon as you begin to run, a little hammer inside swings back and forth each time you take a step. Of course the problem with this is that the pedometer assumes that your stride length is the same every step, so any change of speed is not taken into account. This can lead to a fairly inaccurate reading by the end of the run, but it is a cost effective way to get an idea of the distance you have covered.

GPS The revolution of GPS technology has moved from the car to the runner. Small GPS devices can be attached to the arm and give accurate readings of running speed and distance covered. These devices, like pedometers, are small and unobtrusive, but due to the superior technology they carry a higher price tag. The only minor drawback apart

GPS has evolved from the car to the runner.

from price is that some reports suggest that every now and again the signal can be lost, especially in areas of dense tree cover, leading to a loss of accuracy. Despite this, if you have the budget the GPS systems remain a much more accurate device than pedometers.

Inertial Technology This highly advanced technology is used in aerospace positioning and guidance systems. Like GPS, it provides a highly accurate form of calculating running distance and speed. Polar, Nike and Adidas all sell a form of 'running pod' that is placed on the running shoe and transmits a plethora of information back to a watch receptor. The pod provides data such as running speed, current and average pace per mile (or kilometre), distance travelled, etc. This innovation is perhaps the best all-round running gadget on the market and is certainly well worth the investment.

An inertial running pod.

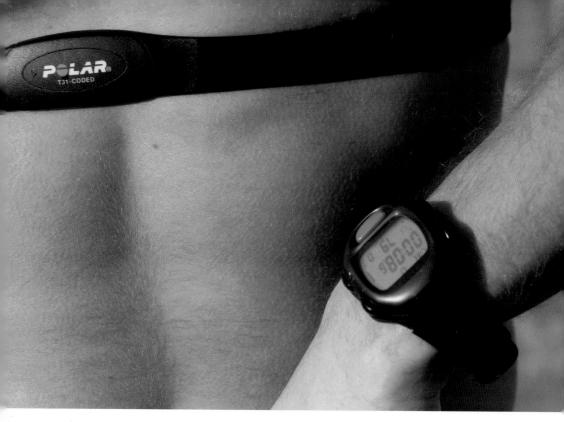

A heart rate monitor strap and watch.

Heart Rate Monitors

Most running experts strongly advise investing in a heart rate monitor as it can be used as an effective tool in charting your training progress. Most models come in two parts, comprising a fabric chest strap and a watch receiver. Different models have varying features, from the top models telling you how fast you are running, to the most basic, which simply display your heart rate. By keeping a note of how hard your heart is working during your training runs you can tell if you are working too hard or not hard enough and how your heart is adapting to your endurance training programme.

Heart monitors are probably the best purchase you can make for your training regime and I strongly advise you to buy one. For more information on how they can be used effectively for training runs, see Chapter 4, which discusses heart rate training in more detail.

Mobile Phone and Panic Alarm

Carrying a mobile phone and/or a panic alarm may seem a little unnecessary, but for some female runners training late at night they offer security and peace of mind. A mobile is certainly useful if you are running a fair distance away from home. Every now and again unexpected problems such as cramp and muscle strains can occur, which can pose a major problem if you are twelve miles away from civilization without any form of communication.

CHAPTER 2

Welcome to Your Body

The physiology of the *active* human body is vastly different from the one sitting down and relaxing in front of the television. As soon as you take your first running stride, a complex series of changes occur in all the major body systems, radically altering the way the body works. Without these changes, you would simply not be able to function.

Many people are aware of the obvious adjustments that take place during a run, such as an increase in heart rate and breathing, but this is just the tip of the iceberg. Contributions from your muscular, skeletal and hormonal (endocrine) systems all play a part in ensuring the active human body runs smoothly.

During your training, all of these physiological processes and adaptations that occur are largely out of your control. Just as you have no direct influence over the fate of your lunch once you have eaten it, to a large extent there is little you can do to directly alter the adaptations that occur during your training.

One thing you *can* do, however, is develop an understanding about the various systems involved so that you are aware of what is happening to your body in the build-up to the big day. Gaining an insight into how everything works will not only make you appreciate the body you have, but also perhaps encourage you to put that extra bit of effort into your sessions to optimize the natural adaptation process.

This chapter will provide you with an understanding of basic exercise physiology. By highlighting all of the significant body systems used whilst running, it offers an insight into some of the 'hows' and 'whys' of endurance training. Although it is not essential that you read this chapter, you may find it useful if you are interested in human adaptation to exercise.

THE CIRCULATORY SYSTEM

Did you know:

- The heart is responsible for circulating the blood through around 60,000 miles (100,000km) of blood vessels.
- The heart beats around 35,000,000 times a year (100,000 times a day).
- The heart pumps 3,600 gallons (about 14,000 litres) of blood around the body every day.
- The resting heart rate of a trained endurance runner can be as low as 35 beats per minute, compared to 80 beats per minute of an untrained runner.

The circulatory system is made up of three main parts, each with a different role to help deliver nutrient rich blood to the working muscles. They are:

- the heart;
- the blood vessels;
- the blood.

The Heart

About the size of a fist, the heart is the 'biological pump' that supplies oxygenated

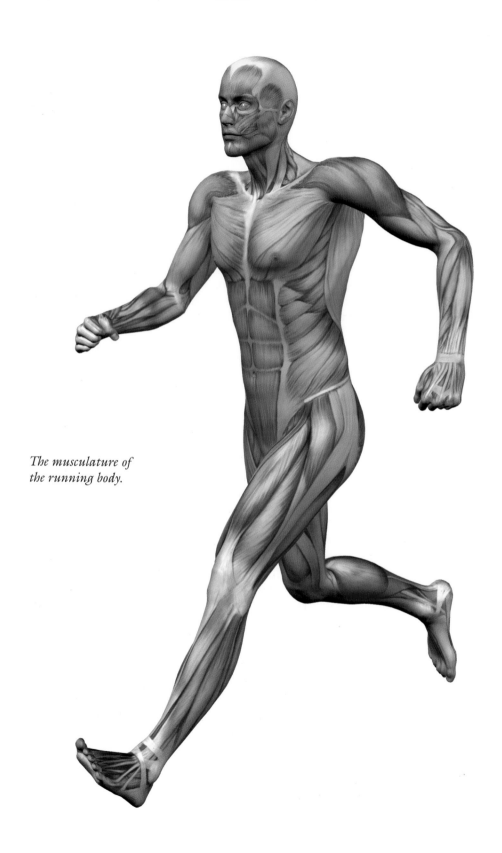

The musculature of the running body.

blood to the working muscles. The more work you ask of your muscles whilst running, the more your heart needs to beat in order to provide the muscles with a sufficient supply of nutrient-rich blood.

Depending on your fitness levels at the start of your training, the amount of blood your heart ejects every beat, or stroke volume (SV), varies greatly:

Subjects	SV at rest (ml)	SV (ml) during maximal exercise
Untrained	55–75	80–110
Trained	80–90	130–150
Elite athlete	100–120	160–220>

(From *Physiology of Sport and Exercise* by Jack H. Wilmore and David L. Costill)

The reason why the stroke volume is low in untrained runners is simply down to the heart having insufficient musculature and therefore strength to pump large amounts of blood with each beat. As a result, the heart needs to beat faster to make up for the low stroke volume if the energy needs of the muscles are to be met. This is the main reason why new runners have a higher running heart rate than more seasoned runners.

The Blood Vessels

Arteries, veins and capillaries form a complex network of blood vessels responsible for transporting blood to and from the heart. Although the arteries and veins are the largest structures, it is the capillaries that play the biggest role during your training, and they undergo dramatic changes as you increase your mileage. The capillaries are tiny blood vessels into which arteries terminate and from which veins begin. During a run, it is through the capillaries that oxygen and other essential nutrients are able to diffuse into the working muscles, and metabolic waste products can be removed and transported away.

As endurance training increases, a process known as *capillarization* occurs, whereby the body is stimulated to manufacture more capillaries in the working muscles to meet the exercise demands. An increase in the number of capillaries not only helps to provide more oxygen and nutrients but also helps to remove waste products far more efficiently. It is because of capillarization that a number of long-distance runs are recommended before a marathon – the body simply needs to be told to manufacture more capillaries

The Blood

Everything that the working muscles need in order to keep running is supplied in the form of blood. The blood contains an array of proteins, vitamins and minerals, all of which are necessary if the body is to keep functioning at an optimum level.

However, blood is not just used as a delivery medium. Metabolic waste products such as lactic acid and carbon dioxide are absorbed by the blood and transported away from the muscles. Without this process, acidity levels in the muscles would increase substantially, making muscular contraction impossible and resulting in severe fatigue.

So it is through the circulatory system that blood can be transported to the working muscles, via a complex network of blood vessels, providing them with sufficient amounts of oxygen and nutrients to initiate and sustain exercise for long periods of time. However, none of these processes would be possible without a constant supply of oxygen, and this task is undertaken by the respiratory system.

THE RESPIRATORY SYSTEM

Did you know:

- During a run, the amount of gas passing in and out of the lungs (pulmonary ventilation) can vary from 256 pints (120 litres)/minute in untrained runners up to a massive 507 pints (240 litres)/minute in highly trained athletes.
- The maximum amount of oxygen that can be inhaled, transported and utilized in the body (VO2 max) can vary from 40ml/kg of body weight/min in untrained runners to 77ml/kg/min in world-class athletes.
- Your left lung is approximately 10 per cent smaller than your right lung.
- The alveoli, which are responsible for gaseous exchange, have a surface area of around 70 square metres – about the size of a volley ball court.

The breathing aspect of running is something many new runners often take a while to get used to. All too often, new runners obsessively focus on their breathing patterns rather than simply letting the body do its job and effectively breathe for you.

In the early stages of a training programme, it is important to undertake some 'walk and jog' sessions, so that you can experience the sensation of increased respiration without feeling the pressure of having to run for the whole session. Adapting your cardiovascular and respiratory systems is a progressive process that takes a little time, so the phrase 'don't run before you can walk' couldn't be more apt.

Working in conjunction with the circulatory system, the respiratory system is needed to breathe in the oxygen from the air into the lungs and expel harmful carbon dioxide from the lungs.

Inspiration

The first stage of oxygen transport begins with the inhalation. Taken in either through the nose or mouth, oxygen travels down the windpipe and enters the lungs. Oxygen is then absorbed by tiny sacs known as alveoli, where it is diffused into the blood; it is at this point that the circulatory system takes over.

It is worth noting that the basic process of inspiration is not significantly different during exercise than at rest. The only notable differences are that during exercise the amount of oxygen taken in is significantly larger and that oxygen is inhaled through the mouth rather than the nose.

It is a common misconception that taking in air through your nose provides more oxygen to the lungs. 'Nose breathing' during heavy exercise, as you can test for yourself, is virtually impossible. As running intensity increases, the body naturally encourages you to breathe through your mouth so that you can take in as much oxygen as possible. The relatively narrow nasal cavity cannot cope with the increased need for air. Breathing in oxygen through the nose simply humidifies the air and reduces the amount of dust particles inhaled.

Expiration

Like inspiration, the basic process of expiration is similar during exercise as it is at rest; the quantity of gaseous exchange is simply larger. Expiration is the process of expelling carbon dioxide from the body. The oxygen that has been transported and utilized by the muscles is changed into deoxygenated blood and carried away through the veins. The diffusion of gases in the alveoli during the expiration process is then reversed from that of inspiration. Carbon dioxide gas diffuses out of the blood and is subsequently expelled out of the nose or mouth.

All this information may be very interesting to a teenager learning human biology, but what relevance does it have to your quest to complete an endurance event? The answer is adaptation. Both your circulatory and respiratory systems will have to adjust considerably if you are to successfully complete your running challenge. Your capillaries, heart and lungs will all undergo significant changes as a result of your training, all of them helping not only your running efficiency but your general state of health too.

THE MUSCULOSKELETAL SYSTEM

Did you know:

- The human body contains over 600 muscles, nine controlling the thumb alone.
- A muscle fibre's use of energy can be over 200 times more during exercise than at rest.
- Elite endurance runners contain around 95 per cent slow twitch muscles in their calf muscles, compared to just 25 per cent in sprinters.

Do you remember all those years ago when you were at school and on sports day every year there was always a handful of your classmates who excelled in one event or another? The same faces did well every year at the 100 meter sprint and invariably, but not always, another group of your peers would excel at the longer distances. At such a young age, these differences in sporting ability did not arise through intensive sports-specific training, but are due to the 'genetic cards' each individual was dealt when they were born.

A number of variances in genetic make-up can help to contribute to athletic success, but the difference in muscle fibre plays a significant role in whether an individual excels in explosive events or longer duration endurance events.

Before the significance of your muscle fibres and how they will influence your training are explained, it is important to first understand the process of movement, how it occurs and how it is fuelled.

> Despite popular belief, a well-designed weight-training programme can not only enable endurance runners to run faster, but can also prevent injury.

The Movement Chemical

Even before you set off for a training run, energy is needed to supply your leg muscles with the ability to move. Ultimately this energy comes from the food we eat but a spaghetti bolognaise, at a muscular level, isn't really of much use. The energy the body needs to produce movement must be supplied in chemical form.

The human body comprises over 600 muscles.

Adenosine tri-phosphate (ATP) is the chemical used to ultimately produce movement. ATP is produced and used in a variety of ways, depending on how much and how quickly energy is needed. During aerobic exercise, such as jogging, ATP is needed to create movement but it is not needed in a hurry, unlike a 100 metre sprint. Therefore, a mixture of carbohydrate and fat are used to produce ATP.

During harder, more intensive training sessions, ATP is needed more quickly in order to meet the instant energy demands. Higher levels of enzymes are then produced to increase the rate of ATP production, along with a quicker breakdown of carbohydrate stores. Fat is a much more complex substance to break down and utilize than carbohydrate, so during your more intensive bouts of training the main fuel source used is carbohydrate.

The Muscle Fibres

When it comes down to the muscles themselves, different types of fibres are called upon, depending on the intensity of exercise being performed.

Our musculature is generally made up of two different types of muscle fibre, which are classed either as slow twitch or as fast twitch, types A and B.

As their names suggest, slow twitch fibres contract relatively slowly and are used for activities that require less explosive movements, such as endurance running. Fast twitch fibres, on the other hand, contract rapidly and are called upon for activities that require fast movements, such as sprinting.

Studies of identical twins have proved that the ratio of muscle fibres we possess is genetically predetermined, suggesting that even before we have taken our first step our inherited muscle fibre ratio will sway us to excel in one sport or another. However, just because someone is born with a higher ratio of fast twitch muscles fibres, it does not necessarily mean that they will be unsuccessful at competing in an endurance event. With sufficient training, research suggests that one fibre type can take on the characteristics of the opposite type.

Slow Twitch

These are the fibres that you will be calling upon during the majority of your training. Predominantly used during long runs, slow twitch fibres are incredibly efficient at oxidizing fat and carbohydrate, producing ample amounts of ATP needed for muscular contraction. Highly aerobic and vascular, it is your slow twitch muscles fibres that need to be trained sufficiently to be able to endure the demands of your long-distance runs.

Fast Twitch

Of the two types of fast twitch fibres, it is the type As that, with training, will work alongside your slow twitch fibres and share the work load on long training runs. The type Bs just sit back and watch them do the work, until a sudden sprint activates them to contract.

When a sudden sprint is initiated, it is your fast twitch muscles that are recruited to work, due to their ability to generate ATP at a quicker rate. At an all-out sprint they are being used at full capacity, not only because of their ability to produce ATP quicker but also because fast twitch fibres are able to contract very quickly.

Do not let the science of fast twitch and slow twitch muscle fibres confuse you. There is still much contradiction in the exercise science community as to the cellular function of muscle fibres, so do not get caught up in the complexity of the subject.

> **It has been proven that one type of muscle fibre is able to take on the characteristics of the other type, in response to specific training.**

THE ENDOCRINE SYSTEM

Did you know:

- Without anti-diuretic hormone (ADH) your urine secretion would rise from 2–4 pints (1–2 litres) a day up to 42 pints (20 litres) a day.
- Your brain is predominantly responsible for regulating your hormones.
- A small deficiency in just one hormone can have a major knock-on effect on other hormones, causing ill health and poor exercise performance.

Although not as obvious to see in action as the other systems, the endocrine system is by no means the least significant. Responsible for the regulation and secretion of hormones, the endocrine system is constantly balancing large numbers of hormones so that the body can be kept in a constant equilibrium. Nine major endocrine glands are responsible for secreting the most important hormones, each playing an individual role in maintaining homeostasis.

When it comes to the regulation of hormones during your training, like all other systems these glands are required to work and respond more rapidly to the continuing changes in oxygen, blood and fluid levels.

Exercise Hormones

Although all hormones are working in one way or another whether at rest or during exercise, whilst training some are needed more than others to allow the body to maintain the level of work you are demanding.

Three hormones are arguably more influential during training than others:

- adrenalin (also known as epinephrine);
- anti-diuretic hormone (ADH);
- insulin.

> A sudden burst of adrenalin into the bloodstream is part of the reason why a 9-year-old boy weighing just 65lb (30kg) managed to lift a 4,100lb (1,860kg) car off his father's chest.

Adrenalin

Also known as epinephrine, adrenalin is responsible for a number of tasks, such as raising heart rate and helping to convert stored carbohydrate (glycogen) into glucose, which is needed to produce ATP.

Although it may appear that we have little control over how adrenalin is utilized, certain conditions and eating habits can have a negative (and positive) effect on our adrenalin levels. Stress, for example, causes adrenalin levels to rise, increasing the heart rate and blood pressure and putting excessive strain on your heart. If prolonged or excessive stress plays a part in your life, it is strongly advisable that you visit your GP or physician regularly throughout the duration of your training programme.

On the other hand, excessive amounts of adrenalin can have a positive effect on exercise performance. This 'fight or flight' hormone can dramatically alter the blood distribution to the muscles and increase their energy output in an instant in times of fear.

It is because of this energy-giving attribute that artificially increasing adrenalin levels has been popular amongst athletes. Adrenalin has such performance-enhancing properties in explosive sports that the drug and doping authorities now ban athletes from taking any product that significantly increases adrenalin levels.

Anti-diuretic Hormone (ADH)

Anti-diuretic hormone is responsible for the regulation of water excretion. Without it, water would simply keep passing through us, making normal life awkward and exercise embarrassing.

You may have noticed whilst exercising that, unless your bladder is excessively full, the necessity to urinate ceases. Even if you begin a run with a slightly full bladder, once ADH levels rise, the kidneys are stimulated to reabsorb water, decreasing the desire to urinate.

As with adrenalin, certain external factors can affect the balance of ADH in the bloodstream. The most common one in this case is alcohol. The diuretic effect of alcohol originates from the fact that it inhibits the secretion of ADH, resulting in an increased desire to urinate more regularly. Over the course of an evening, alcohol causes the body to loose large quantities of fluid from the cells, leading to dehydration and heavily contributing to the dreaded hangover. Dehydration has an incredibly detrimental effect on your body with regards to your running, and therefore drinking binges are not advisable – especially the evening before a training run.

Insulin

As far as exercise is concerned, insulin is key to ensuring that the glucose level of the blood remains within appropriate limits. If insulin levels are off balance – either too high or too low – running performance can be impaired.

Insulin is secreted by the pancreas every time carbohydrate is consumed. The insulin is then responsible for storing away that carbohydrate in the liver and muscles in the form of glycogen, or keeping it in the bloodstream in the form of glucose to stabilize blood sugar levels.

The exact amount secreted is dependent not only on the type of carbohydrate eaten but also on our biochemical individuality. It is estimated that around 75 per cent of the population secrete excessive amounts of insulin. This can cause too much carbohydrate to be stored away, leaving insufficien amounts in the bloodstream.

During exercise, the body is generally abl to regulate insulin levels well. With training cell adaptation occurs, making them mor responsive to insulin and reducing the need fo it. Potential problems can still arise, however if your management of carbohydrate type an timing before a run is poor. If insulin level are raised too high in the moments leadin up to a race or training run, it can push bloo sugar levels down. This can leave you feelin exhausted and lacklustre without even takin one stride.

THE IMMUNE SYSTEM

Did you know:

- Every day your immune system fight millions of potentially harmful bacteri without you even knowing about it.
- Over 52 elite American athletes missed th Barcelona Olympics because of illness o infection.
- In runners, studies indicate that infection cause more days off training than injuries.

Another system we completely take fo granted is the immune system. The onl time we are really aware it is there is when w contract an infection and can feel our gland swell, usually under the jaw or under th arms. Every day we fight invisible microbes which our body absorbs and kills without u even knowing about it.

It is a known fact that elite enduranc runners are more susceptible to contractin a cold than most people. This is due to th fact that in the hours after a run, the immun system is temporarily depressed and open t invading microbes. Even though you may no necessarily regard yourself as an elite runne you too will also be more at risk of getting a infection during your training.

> **Many runners choose to use potent vitamin C tablets to help protect and boost their immune system from the common cold.**

Strong evidence suggests that the reason for the immunosuppressive effects of exercise is down to the rise of *catecholamines* and *gluco-corticoids* in the bloodstream. It is suggested that one way of combating this is to ensure that carbohydrates are consumed during training in an attempt to attenuate this rise.

Now that you are a little more informed as to how the body is going to react to training, you are ideally placed to learn about the actual running itself. Although you may be running at one constant pace in a long-distance event, the intensity at which you need to train to be well prepared is anything but constant. The next chapter outlines the varying degrees of running intensity and why altering your pace during training can help you prepare for a quick race.

CHAPTER 3

Running Intensity

Before you embark on your endurance training regime, it is important to understand the reasons why you need to vary the types and intensity of your training runs. Effective endurance running is more than simply going for a jog a few times a week and upping the mileage every now and again. Injury prevention, adaptation and enhanced enjoyment are just some of the reasons why your training needs to vary from day to day and week to week.

EXERCISE INTENSITY

In 2005 rower James Cracknell, the two times British Olympic gold medallist, decided to trade in his oars for a pair of running shoes and attempt the London Marathon. With the help of a friend experienced in endurance training, James had to radically adapt his training philosophy. After being used to train for an event that lasts for around six minutes, he reportedly had problems altering his training philosophy to a lower intensity for an event that would take him three hours. Though injury ruled him out in 2005, he completed the course in 2006 in three hours, just months after rowing across the Atlantic.

By adopting correct training methods at the correct intensity, you will adapt your body to make the motion of running as effortless as possible, creating improved efficiency and energy economy. This adaptation can be stimulated through different types of training intensity but getting the correct balance of training in your weekly running timetable is

trickier than you may think. If the intensity you train at is too low (under-training), then the process of adaptation will be insufficient to help you make progress. Under-training means you are:

- completing your long runs too slowly for your desired race finishing time;
- running your interval sessions too slowly to encourage adaptation;
- failing to adequately increase your weekly mileage;
- running too infrequently.

On the other hand, if your training intensity is too high, you are more susceptible to injury and symptoms of over-training may crop up. Over-training means you are:

- completing your long runs too fast increasing your chances of injury;
- running your interval sessions too hard placing excessive stress on joints and tendons;
- increasing your weekly mileage too fast not allowing the body time to adapt;
- running too frequently.

Both over-training and under-training can severely hamper your progress. Inadvertently favouring one or the other is clearly detrimental. In my experience, the majority of people training for an endurance event tend to over-train rather than under-train. When it comes to long-distance running, less is sometimes more.

A high-intensity training session.

> By constantly changing the type of training you do, you can avoid hitting a plateau and can keep improving your fitness levels.

AEROBIC, ANAEROBIC AND VO2 MAX TRAINING

When we run, we have the option of running at different speeds. As a general rule the quicker we run the less time we are able to run for, as fatigue quickly sets in. Over the course of your training, it is important to perform your runs at a variety of speeds to encourage different types of adaptation. Running long distances at a slow and comfortable pace will help you to improve running endurance whilst a quicker pace will help you not only improve your overall running speed but also improve the body's efficiency at removing metabolic waste products. The different speeds that you train at can be placed into three main categories:

- aerobic threshold;
- anaerobic threshold;
- VO2 max.

Aerobic Threshold

Generally speaking, all exercise performed at a steady rate, such as walking or jogging, is classed as aerobic exercise. Aerobic exercise is fuelled by the oxidation of fats and carbohydrates. At this intensity, the body is easily able to take in, transport and utilize oxygen and supply it to the working muscles in sufficient amounts that the energy sources (predominantly carbohydrate and fat) can be oxidized and used to fuel movement. The majority of your training will take the form of aerobic exercise, not only to stimulate cardiovascular adaptation but also to encourage the process of capillarization.

The best way to tell if you are jogging in an aerobic state is to do the talking test. If you can jog and speak a sentence before needing to take a breath, then you are training aerobically.

As your jogging pace increases and talking in sentences becomes difficult, it indicates that you are reaching the limit of your aerobic threshold. As the intensity increases further, running can begin to feel a little bit more 'uncomfortable'. This is the point at which you slowly begin to enter into anaerobic training.

*Pushing each other to go faster
is a great motivator.*

A comfortably paced aerobic run.

Anaerobic Threshold

Once the intensity of a run increases to
your anaerobic threshold, the ability to talk
without regular breaths becomes very diffi
cult. Training in your anaerobic threshold
causes acidity levels in your muscles to rise
causing your heart rate to increase to help
clear the lactic acid. Running anaerobically is
very hard and uncomfortable to maintain for
long periods of time.

Technically speaking, running in your
anaerobic threshold is the highest intensity
that you can maintain, without your lactic
acid levels rising too high. If your pace or
the intensity of your run continue to rise
lactic acid levels become too overwhelming
for your muscles and fatigue forces you to
stop.

Highly trained runners are able to tolerate
running within their anaerobic threshold for
long periods of time, but less fit runners may

OPPOSITE: *Anaerobic running
requires more concentration.*

ind that just five minutes is tough work. With
ufficient and specific training, it is possible
o build up a tolerance to perform exercise at
his intensity for longer, not only improving
our anaerobic fitness, but also your aerobic
itness. This is one of the reasons why both
ntensities of exercise need to be undertaken
or an endurance event.

VO2 Max

The term VO2 max is often bandied around
n fitness circles, with many people not really
understanding what it means. Although the
erm may look like part of a quadratic equa-
ion, it is actually very simple to understand.

Put simply, your VO2 max is the *maximum
amount of oxygen your body is able to take in,
transport and utilize*. It is expressed as ml/
g/min. Or in plain English:

*Millilitres (of oxygen) per kg of (body weight)
per minute (of work performed)*

Your maximal oxygen uptake takes place very
lose to your maximum heart rate (HR max),
o when you are at or very close to exercising
t your maximum capacity it can be said that
you are training at your VO2 max. This level
of work can obviously only be performed for
 short period of time before fatigue sets in.

Understanding or knowing your own VO2
max is not an essential part of endurance
training for the majority of runners. It may
be of interest to those runners who are fasci-
nated by statistics and running physiology,
but if you are competing in your first race
do not concern yourself too much with VO2
max, and do not let it over-complicate your
training regime.

> Former marathon world record holder
> Alberto Salazar had a recorded VO2 max of
> 70ml/kg/min. Experts were baffled, and
> suggested his marathon time of 2 hours,
> 6 minutes should result in a much higher
> VO2 max. It was discovered that he was
> beating his rivals, all with far superior VO2
> max levels, because he was able to maintain
> a running speed at an impressive 86 per cent
> of VO2 max.
>
> To put all this in perspective, to date the
> highest recorded maximum oxygen uptake
> is that of a cross-country skier, who was
> recorded to have a VO2 max of a massive
> 94ml/kg/min.

It is worth pointing out that a runner with
a high VO2 max does not necessarily have
a superior level of fitness compared with a
runner with a lower VO2 max. Although
the ability to take in, transport and utilize
more oxygen than a competitor may appear
to be an advantage, studies suggest that some
athletes are able to maintain exercise at a
higher percentage of their VO2 max than a
runner with a higher VO2 max.

If you are interested in finding out what
your VO2 max is, the best way is to seek
advice from a fitness professional at a gym,
so you can have peace of mind that you
will be tested safely and accurately. Whether
you wish to regularly review your VO2 max
status or just check up on it every now and
again, remember to keep all the figures
and terms in perspective. You may have an
impressive VO2 max, but come the last mile
of a race when your legs are screaming at you
to stop, mental strength overtakes maximal
oxygen uptake as a means to get you across
that finishing line.

OPPOSITE: VO2 max training is tough – you need to be 100 per cent focused.

CHAPTER 4

Listen to Your Heart

Heart rate training is a great way to keep track of your progress.

The subject of heart rate training is vast, resulting in a number of books being published on the subject. The following pages aim to point out the basics of heart rate training and the changes you should look out for as your fitness levels improve.

Keeping an eye on how your heart responds during training and rest should form an integral part of your routine. Your heart is the pump that provides all the essential nutrients to your muscles, and making sure it is responding to training the way it should is strongly recommended.

There are some 'old school' runners who unequivocally condemn the use of heart rate monitors for training and racing. Dismissing them as a waste of time and money, some people believe they can actually have a detrimental effect on training by encouraging a runner to run by heart rate alone and not by feeling.

Although this view is not held by the majority of running experts, it is certainly worth bearing in mind that heart rate training is to be used as a guide, especially in a race situation. It would seem nothing short of crazy if, in a race situation, you slowed your pace down in the closing 800 metres of the race, just because you noticed you are running at your maximum heart rate. Mental strength in a race situation is far more of a determining factor than a number flashing at you from your wrist receiver.

Modern technology makes measuring your heart rate during training both easy and inexpensive. Gone are the days when you needed to place a sweaty finger on your wrist and struggle to accurately count the beats. Heart rate monitors now transmit information from a fabric strap that fits comfortably around the chest directly to a watch receiver on your wrist.

There is a wide range of heart rate monitors on the market, with an equally wide range of price tags. Ideally, you should choose a monitor that includes a stopwatch function, so you can record how long your runs take, along with an average heart rate function, making fitness improvements easier to monitor.

Keeping an eye on the way your heart rate responds to exercise can help your training immeasurably, by effectively telling you if your fitness levels are improving or stagnating. Equally, at rest with your feet up on the couch, your heart rate can tell you if you are making fitness improvements, or even if you are training too hard.

RESTING HEART RATE (RHR)

The heart at rest generally beats anywhere between sixty and eighty beats per minute (bpm), with women boasting a slightly higher RHR than men. As your fitness levels improve and your heart gets stronger, the amount of blood ejected with each beat (stroke volume) increases, resulting in the heart needing to beat less often. Many elite athletes have resting heart rates well below 50bpm, some even as low as the mid-20s. Genetics also play a key role in determining RHR, so just because an individual possesses a low heart rate at rest this does not necessarily mean that it is because they possess the physical abilities of an elite athlete.

Heart rate straps are comfortable and fully adjustable.

Measuring heart rate the old-fashioned way.

Measuring Resting Heart Rate

Due to natural (and unnatural) fluctuations in resting heart rate, it is important to be consistent when you take a reading. The best time to take a RHR reading is first thing in the morning, as soon as you wake up. Not only does this make repeat readings more accurate by being taken at the same time each day, but also no other external factors can influence a false reading.

The easiest way to take it is to strap on your heart rate monitor, lie down and measure your heart rate for about five minutes. As long as your monitor has an 'average heart rate' function, you will then easily be able to recall the information and log it in a diary.

If you do not have a heart monitor, simply find the point of your strongest pulse, which is usually found on your wrist (radial) or under your jaw (carotid). Use a watch or timer to then count the number of beats you feel in thirty seconds and then double it. You then have the figure for your RHR.

If you make a point of recording your RHR once a week, you will begin to notice a gradual decrease in heart rate, proving that your fitness levels are improving.

Reasons for an elevated RHR

Every now and again, you may notice a slight elevation in your resting heart rate. A number of factors can influence your resting heart rate, so to ensure it is measured accurately you must be aware of the most common reasons why it can fluctuate.

Adrenalin
As mentioned in the previous chapter, the hormone adrenalin has a direct effect on your heart and can increase its output enormously. The main causes of excessive adrenalin secretion are:

- caffeine intake;
- anticipation of exercise;
- stress.

Caffeine stimulates the adrenal glands to secrete an increased quantity of adrenalin, especially in those who do not consume it regularly. As a result, a harmless cup of coffee half an hour before a RHR test can produce an inaccurate, elevated reading.

The anticipation of exercise is often understated but highly influential on the heart at rest. I have witnessed a client's heart rate rise from 100 bpm to 150 bpm in around three minutes, by sitting still and focusing on performing an intense 500m sprint on a rowing ergometer.

Increased stress levels provoke a prolonged elevation in adrenalin levels, causing the heart to beat higher at rest than it should. If you feel you are unduly stressed, it is advisable to have regular medical check-ups.

Illness
An unexplained increase in resting heart rate can be an excellent way of foreseeing the symptoms of an illness. Experienced runners who regularly keep in touch with their RHR can often anticipate that they are about to come down with a virus such as a cold, simply by noticing an increase of around 10bpm in resting and exercising heart rate. If you are finding a run noticeably tougher than usual, and your heart rate is higher than you'd expect, there is a strong possibility you will be reaching for the tissues in a couple of days.

Warm Environment
An increase in environmental temperature can affect your heart at rest as well as during exercise. If the body is exposed to a temperature it is not used to, blood is diverted closer to the skin where it can cool down, resulting in an increased heart rate.

World champion triathlete Tim Don.

Other Factors

If your RHR remains higher than usual for a prolonged period, or you feel it is higher than it should be and none of the factors above are applicable, it is strongly advised that you get yourself checked out medically. There are other reasons for an increased RHR, most of which may require medical intervention – elevated blood calcium levels and increased thyroid hormone secretion, for example, both increase RHR and require medical treatment. It is also worth noting that in some cases certain medications may be responsible for artificially raising heart rate, a situation worth discussing with your doctor.

Reasons for a low RHR

People with a low RHR also often suffer from low blood pressure. Though not necessarily a problem, short-lived symptoms of dizziness and light-headiness can occur when standing up quickly from a lying or seated position, which can become a bit of an annoyance – especially when people automatically assume you have been drinking.

Generally speaking, there are fewer common reasons for a RHR to be abnormally low. Although increasing your fitness levels will significantly lower your rate, this is certainly not detrimental to your health. Medication can once again strongly influence cardiac response. Beta blockers or pills for hypertension can cause a low heart rate, so if you are on such medication care must be taken.

A prolonged period of a slow resting heart rate along with symptoms of lethargy and fatigue should also be checked out. These possible symptoms of hypothyroidism can go on for months without diagnosis. If your training is harder than you think and you feel under the weather, it is certainly worth getting yourself looked at by your doctor.

MAXIMUM HEART RATE (HR MAX)

The best way to accurately discover your true maximum heart rate is not really much fun. To find out the maximum number of times your heart will beat in a minute requires you to exercise to complete exhaustion, not only taxing you physically but also requiring a lot of mental strength.

Most maximum heart rate tests are performed in a controlled environment, usually on a treadmill, exercise bike or rowing machine. Regardless of which mode you use, the chances are that the test will not be complete until you fall off your chosen machine and writhe around on the floor gasping for air. Sounds tempting, doesn't it?

Fortunately, there is an easier way to find out your maximum heart rate without subjecting yourself to what feels like a near-death experience. To find out your *theoretical* maximum heart rate all you need to do is simply subtract your age from 220. For example:

If you are 40 years old: 220 - 40 = 180

Training in the heat elevates your heart rate.

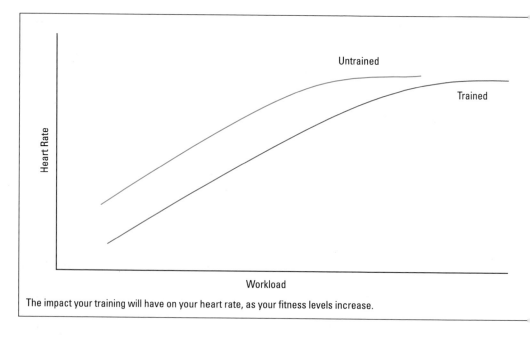

The impact your training will have on your heart rate, as your fitness levels increase.

Therefore, theoretically the maximum number of times your heart can beat in one minute is 180 times.

Unfortunately, as with many principles in this book, individuality plays such a signifi-cant role that it makes this theory potentially useless. This formula is very useful as a guide, but in reality I have found very few people for whom it is accurate.

For many runners, especially those in their more 'mature' years, they are able to run along quite happily with a rate well above their theoretical maximum. In fact according to leading sports physiologists David Costill and Jack Wilmore:

- 68 per cent of 40-year-olds have an actual maximum heart rate of between 168 and 192 bpm;
- 95 per cent of 40-year-olds have a maximum heart rate in the range of 156–192 bpm.

This does *not*, however, mean that you should ignore your theorized maximum heart rate and embark on a run with the intent of proving it wrong. As a general rule, the younger you are the more likely it is tha this formula will apply to you. If you notice during a hard session that your heart rate exceeds your theoretical maximum, adjust i accordingly.

TRAINING HEART RATE

Once you have an idea of your maximum hear rate, you are now in a position to work ou the heart rate zones you should be training a for the various intensities of running – aerobi or anaerobic.

Your heart rate during a run is essentially a measurement of the demand placed on the cardio-respiratory system to deliver suffi-cient levels of oxygen and nutrients to the working muscles so that exercise intensity car be maintained. Over time, as a result of your training, your heart will adapt to the stresse being asked of it, making it more efficient and able to tolerate a workload you once found difficult.

With the correct training plan, your heart will respond to training in a very simila manner to that in the graph above. Not only

Aerobic threshold training should feel comfortable.

Aerobic Threshold Heart Rate

Running within your aerobic threshold will take up the majority of your training. Even on race day, for the half and full marathons your heart should beat within the aerobic zone until the closing stages of the race. However, the more conditioned you are, the closer to your aerobic threshold you will be able to run.

Working out your aerobic threshold heart rate is very simple, although if you read too many books on the subject you are likely to get very confused. Due to the enormous differences in fitness levels and individuality, coming up with a generic figure is impossible. It appears that many 'experts' simply cannot agree on the best way to determine accurately your aerobic threshold, but you can get a rough idea.

If we use the previous example of a runner with a maximum heart rate of 180, then their aerobic threshold heart rate generally falls somewhere between 70 and 75 per cent of their HR max.

Aerobic threshold heart rate for a runner with a HR max of 180 is:

70 per cent of 180 = 126
75 per cent of 180 = 134

Aerobic threshold HR is therefore between 126 and 134.

This clearly demonstrates the large range in which your aerobic threshold heart rate can fall. By calculating your aerobic threshold using these percentages alone, you run the risk of training either with a heart rate that is too high, leading to premature fatigue, or

will your heart not need to work nearly as hard at a given workload but you will also be able to sustain a run at a workload that you would have previously found impossible.

A training programme suited to your training goal is explained in much greater detail in chapters 7 and 8, but first it is important to work out the heart rate zones you should be training in for the various intensities of running – aerobic or anaerobic.

Anaerobic threshold training is tough – but worth it.

too low, in which case your fitness will not improve.

My suggested approach to finding your aerobic threshold heart rate is to embark on a short jog on a flat route for around ten to fifteen minutes (or a swift walk if your fitness levels are low). Wear your heart rate monitor and settle down into a pace that you would regard as 'comfortable'. Understandably, to many people 'comfortable' means sitting in front of the TV with the cat on your lap, but in running terms it simply means a pace that you feel you could sustain for a 'reasonable length of time', and a pace whereby you can converse with someone without needing to gasp for air after every word.

Throughout the fifteen minutes, glance at your heart rate every now and again and you will notice that after a while your heart rate should level off and tick along at a fairly even rate. As long as you remain 'comfortable' and you are able to talk in brief sentences this is your aerobic threshold heart rate, falling anywhere between 70 and 75 per cent of your HR max. Remember that your heart is different to anyone else's so making comparisons to a friend's or training partner's heart rate is a waste of time.

Anaerobic Threshold Heart Rate

When your running speed begins to creep up and running no longer feels as comfortable as it did in your aerobic zone, this suggests that you are edging towards your anaerobic threshold. Remember that this intensity is the level at which lactic acid begins to increase significantly and the body has to work hard to remove it; run much quicker above your anaerobic threshold and exercise starts to become impossible to sustain. Throughout the course of your training programme, you will be performing numerous 'anaerobic training' sessions for the reasons outlined previously. On this basis, it is a good idea to know what your anaerobic threshold heart rate is.

Running anaerobically is a very different sensation to running aerobically. Holding a conversation in words, let alone short sentences, is very difficult and more concentration is required to maintain the increased intensity.

Fitness levels again determine how long a runner can sustain exercise in their anaerobic zone, but for well-conditioned runners exercise bouts of over an hour can be sustained anaerobically. Once the anaerobic threshold is reached, lactic acid in the muscles will eventually become too much and running will be impossible after a short while. It is generally regarded that your anaerobic threshold heart rate occurs at approximately 85 to 90 per cent of your HR max.

Anaerobic threshold heart rate for a runner with a HR max of 192 is:

85 per cent of 192 = 163
90 per cent of 192 = 172

Anaerobic threshold HR is therefore between 163 and 172.

If percentages are now beginning to bug you, by adding twenty to thirty beats to your aerobic threshold heart rate you should have a pretty good estimation of your anaerobic threshold.

Runners often dread anaerobic threshold training sessions, because of the discomfort levels experienced. The fitness gains that can be made through effective anaerobic training, however, are substantial. Over time, you will notice that you will be able to exercise for longer at your anaerobic threshold, without lactic acid levels building up uncontrollably. This will be especially noticeable for new runners. You may find that at the beginning of your training, a run at your anaerobic threshold heart rate may last for just five minutes before lactic acid levels become excessively high. After a series of training runs, outlined later, your tolerance will increase dramatically, making it possible for you to run anaerobically for longer periods of time.

The increased tolerance to a higher workload is clearly significant to a runner if their aspiration is to improve their time over the half or full marathon. The training might be tough but the feeling of achievement once you cross the finishing line is something that money can't buy.

CARDIOVASCULAR DRIFT

The process of cardiovascular drift is certainly one that our 'old school' runners would use as an example as to why heart rate training could confuse some runners. Cardiovascular drift is a process whereby a runner's heart rate will slowly increase over a long period of time, despite running at the same intensity.

It is believed that the main cause of cardiovascular drift is the body heating up. Excess bodily heat needs to be controlled to maintain optimum and safe exercise conditions. As a

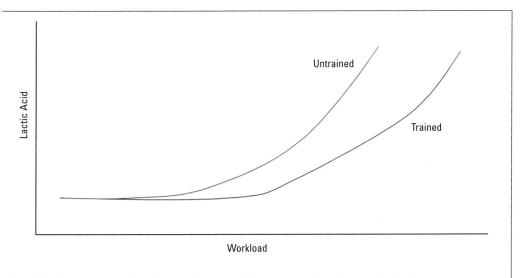

The relationships between lactic acid accumulation and different training intensities, in trained and untrained runners.

Suggested Training Heart Rates (Guide)		
Age	*Aerobic (70%)*	*Anaerobic (85%)*
20	140	170
30	133	161
40	126	153
50	119	**144**
60	112	**136**
70	105	**127**

Note: These values are approximate and may very well need to be adapted as you progress through your training programme. The areas highlighted in bold are certainly likely to be higher, but always err on the side of caution.

result, it is thought that over time blood is diverted to the skin in an effort to lose excess body heat, making less blood available for the working muscles. In order to maintain the required intensity the heart rate must increase to meet the demands of the body's internal cooling system and the working muscles. This theory has been challenged, but to be honest the scientific reason for cardiovascular drift is not particularly important. The important point for the runner is to be aware of its existence and understand that heart rate does not remain at a constant level over the duration of a long run. Although there is very little that can be done to stop cardiovascular drift, the importance of sufficient hydration to keep the body cool is evident.

KEEP A NOTE

Measuring your heart rate during your training clearly has major benefits and can aid your performance. However, it is important to remember that it should only be used as a guideline – following your heart rate too stringently could make your training too one dimensional and leave you under-trained.

It is a good idea to make a note of your heart rate statistics in your training diary and jot down on a scale of one to ten how hard the run felt, one being easy, ten being lung-bustingly difficult. This way you can refer back to them throughout the training regime and keep a close eye on how you are progressing. Not only is it satisfying noticing how well your heart rate is adapting, but it can equally show up any potential shortfalls.

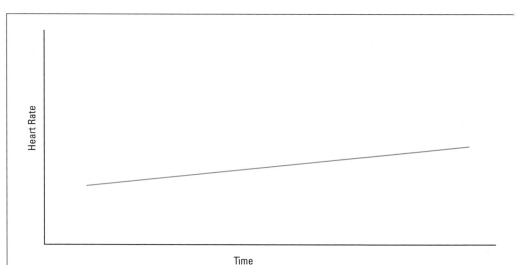

A runner experiencing cardiovascular drift would show a gradual, steady increase in their heart rate over time.

CHAPTER 5

Stretching and Core Stability

Every now and again, newspaper supplements and magazines feature articles about the pros and cons of stretching. Headlines such as 'A new study suggests that stretching is a waste of time' are fairly typical. You could spend hours studying the research and still be none the wiser as to whether stretching should form part of your training.

It goes without saying that over the course of the next few months your leg muscles are going to be getting their fair share of abuse. Although your arms are important to help propel you forwards, it is the muscles in your legs that take a lot of strain and will be ultimately responsible for getting you across the finishing line.

Due to our unique genetic make-up, certain muscles are more susceptible to injury than others. Pelvic imbalances, varying stride length and running gait variances are all reasons why one group of leg muscles may take more strain than others.

Irrespective of the research, I always advise anyone partaking in any form of exercise to stretch beforehand, the philosophy simply being that even if studies suggest that it may not be necessary, it certainly will not do any harm.

PREPARING THE MUSCLES FOR STRETCHING

Stretches are generally performed to elongate the muscles and prepare them for exercise. However, if performed incorrectly injuries can occur. The most common mistake people make when stretching out muscles is failing to warm them up first. Muscles are like clay in the way they react to warmth. When cold, muscles are less pliable and can snap more easily if they are stretched too vigorously. However, once they have warmed up with the help of increased blood flow, they become a lot more supple and are less vulnerable to tearing.

To ensure that there is adequate blood flow to the muscles, it is important to go for a short power walk or very light jog for a few minutes to stimulate the blood flow before you begin to stretch. Once your legs have warmed up, you can then begin to perform very light stretches to begin to prepare the muscles for training.

THE STRETCHES

The following pages illustrate a variety of stretches for the major running muscles. Each stretch should be performed gently at first and can be gradually increased in intensity for subsequent stretches. The following procedures should be followed for every stretch:

- Stretch out each muscle a minimum of two times, increasing the stretch slightly every time.
- Hold each stretch for about 15–20 seconds.
- Avoid over-stretching the muscle; it is not a competition. Hold the stretch when you feel the tension begin to significantly increase.

A quad stretch.

A hamstring stretch.

- Do not 'bounce' the muscles. This is known as ballistic stretching and is best avoided. You have little control over the stretch and one centimetre too far can mean a torn muscle.
- Make stretching before and after a run part of the routine. Keeping the muscles stretched can help reduce your chances of injury.

The major muscles you need to stretch are:

- the quadriceps;
- the hamstrings;
- the adductors (inside of the leg);
- the hip flexors;
- the glutes;
- the calves;
- the illio tibial band (ITB).

The Quadriceps

- Take hold of the middle of your foot, and bring your heel towards your bottom, making sure that the upper part of your bent leg is level with the other one.
- The stabilizing leg should be slightly bent at the knee.
- As your foot gets closer to your bottom, your quad muscles should being to feel like they are being stretched. If you do not feel a stretch, tilt your pelvis upwards, whilst maintaining the same position.
- Hold the stretch for 15–20 seconds then change legs.

The Hamstrings

- Extend the leg you want to stretch 30 centimetres or so in front of you, keeping it straight.
- Gently place your hands on the other leg at about thigh level and slowly bend it from the knee, as though you were about to sit down on a chair.

OPPOSITE: Stretching is vital to help prevent injuries.

- Do not bend your back – keep it as straight as you can. You will begin to feel a stretch in the hamstring muscles as you lower yourself down.
- Once you feel the stretch, hold it for 15–20 seconds then change legs.
- If you want to get an extra stretch in the calf muscle, slowly lift your foot upwards.

The Adductors

- Face forwards and extend one leg to the side with your foot angling 45 degrees away from you. The other leg must remain straight and the foot pointing forwards.
- Slowly shift your weight to the side of the bent leg and you will begin to feel a stretch on the inside of the straight leg.
- Ensure your hips are facing forwards at all times. Hold the stretch for 15–20 seconds.

Hip Flexors

- This stretch can be performed with the rear leg straight (as illustrated) or bent.
- Face forwards and take a large step, keeping the rear leg straight or bent on the floor.
- Keep your trunk upright and push your hips forward to feel the stretch in the hip flexor muscles at the top of the straight leg.
- Hold for 15–20 seconds then change legs.

A stretch for the adductors (groin).

Glutes

This is an excellent stretch for your major gluteal muscles.

- Lie on your back and bend both legs 90 degrees at the hips and knees.
- Place the ankle of the side you wish to stretch on the knee of the opposite leg.
- Grab hold of the leg you are not stretching and slowly pull it towards you.
- You will feel a stretch in the buttock of the other leg. Hold for 15–20 seconds and change legs.

If you have access to a gym ball, you can perform a similar stretch. Adopt the same leg position and drop your glutes towards the ground to feel the stretch.

Calves

- Stand up straight and place the calf you want to stretch behind you.
- With your hands on your hips, or leaning against a wall or tree slowly lean forwards, ensuring you rear heel stays in contact with the ground.

ITB

- Using a wall for balance, place the leg you want to stretch behind you and away from the wall.
- Keep the other leg slightly bent at the knee.
- If you don't feel a stretch, laterally move your hips towards the wall, keeping both legs stationary.
- Keep in mind that unless your ITB is very tight, you may not feel a stretch.

A hip flexor stretch.

A gluteal and piriformis stretch.

A piriformis stretch using a gym ball.

A calf stretch – keep the heel on the ground.

Stretching the ITB.

CORE STABILITY

Core stability is now regarded as an important and necessary part of a runner's training. Many experts believe that by keeping your core muscles strong you can avoid injury and give yourself a far better chance of tolerating the demands of endurance training.

What is the Core?

The core is effectively your body, minus your arms and legs. As much of a paradox as this may sound when you are training for a running event, a strong core is essential to keep your body stable during a running motion, and it can help avoid placing stress on your skeletal structures.

The Core and Training

Exercise disciplines such as Pilates place a lot of emphasis on core strength and although the majority of your training should naturally be in the form of running, the occasional Pilates class will hold you in good stead to help keep the major core muscles strong. If you have difficulty finding the time to attend classes, try these simple exercises to help strengthen your core.

The Plank
- Adopt a press-up position but rest on your forearms rather than your hands.
- If the position is uncomfortable, drop to your knees but keep your back straight.
- Keeping your back straight, hold this position for 30 seconds.
- Repeat the exercise five times, increasing the duration as your core strength improves.
- To further challenge the core muscles, use a stability ball as illustrated opposite.
- If you feel discomfort in your lower back, cease the exercise immediately.

The Plank on a Stability Ball
Performing the plank on the stability ball can be extremely taxing, and care must be taken. Feel free to rest on your knees rather than your feet if you find it too difficult. As

Core strength – the plank.

Core strength – the plank on the stability ball.

your core muscles become stronger, try the following progressions, always keeping your body still and only moving the arms:

- Move the ball forwards and backwards.
- Move the ball side-to-side.
- Draw circles with the ball.
- Write your name with the ball.
- Write the alphabet with the ball.

The importance of keeping your core muscles strong throughout your training should certainly not be overlooked, but there is no need to get carried away. Performing these exercises twice a week is sufficient to maintain good core stability.

There is a wide range of other exercises that help strengthen your core, so if you feel you would benefit from further advice it is advisable to consult with a fitness professional.

CHAPTER 6

The Training Part 1: The Importance of Variety

Adding variety to your regime is an integral part of your training. Contrary to popular belief, effective marathon training does not simply involve running at one constant pace and upping the mileage every week or so.

A number of variations can be added to a training programme that not only add variety to your runs, but also allow your cardiovascular system to adapt better. Sticking to one form of training not only makes your race preparations tedious and boring, but you are also less likely to make the fitness gains required to meet your running goals.

This chapter will explain the different types of training runs you should be undertaking and, more importantly, it will explain why you should be doing them. By understanding how a certain type of training improves your running, you are much better placed to alter the training programme outlined later, to suit your specific lifestyle and weekly routine.

KEEPING IT SIMPLE

14 miles alternating 2× current MP/1× recovery @ MP +45secs, after a long warm-up and with a long cool-down for a total 7 miles @ MP.

Irrespective of the training run you are doing, it is important to keep it simple. The above training run was found somewhere on the Internet, seemingly trying to confuse the reader as much as possible. Examples like

this are fairly typical in training regimes and often unnecessarily over-complicate things. Training is hard enough without needing to decode a cryptic session such as the one above.

If you are a new runner, it is so important to avoid getting overwhelmed by complicated training sessions and phraseology, and instead concentrate on basic training runs. As you become more advanced, you will slowly be able to decode and relate to cryptic-looking descriptions of training sessions, but keeping training simple ensures your runs are taxing the body and not your brain.

THE TRAINING RUNS

Although you may be able to successfully complete your chosen event with a small selection of training types, it is advisable to keep altering your training stimuli by including most, if not all, of the following training types. By constantly changing the way you perform your sessions, your fitness levels are far less likely to plateau and you are less likely to get bored with the same runs week in, week out.

Above all, remember that endurance training is not an exact science. Unlike applied mathematics where there is only one correct answer, when it comes to the human body the variances are massive. There is every chance a first-time endurance runner could

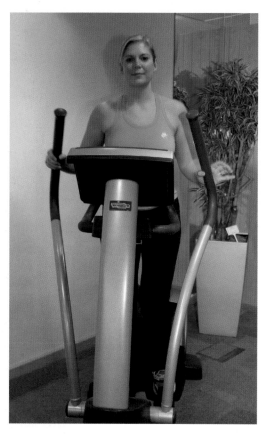

Keep your training varied.

Whether you are training for a half or full marathon, a steady run generally speaking is just below your race pace. If you are using a heart rate monitor for your training runs, your heart should be beating in the region of 65–75 per cent of your HRM for steady runs, although for experienced runners competing in half marathons a higher heart rate is common, as they are able to tolerate a higher work rate for longer periods.

Steady runs form a large part of training, as this is about the pace that you should be aiming for during your distance runs. It will not take long for you to become accustomed to the feeling of your comfortable pace, and with time you will be able know to within ten to fifteen seconds when you have run a mile or a kilometre.

During training runs at a steady pace, it is an idea every now and again to increase your pace for a few miles, just to see how you tolerate a quicker run. By experimenting during training and learning what your body is capable of, you will be in a much better position on race day to know what you can get away with. Fatiguing too early in a race frustrates so many runners every year, as most of the time the reason is simply that they went off too fast and only have themselves to blame. To avoid falling into the same trap, purposely over-pace a steady pace training run and see how you feel. For example, if the extra pace elevates your heart rate to 85 per cent HRM and you are feeling pretty tired, then you know that this pace from the start of a race is too fast.

By finding out as much as you can about your body and its running ability in training, you will be better placed and informed during the race itself. This knowledge will ultimately give you confidence about your running capability, leading to a far more enjoyable race experience.

finish a race in an incredibly quick time, not having done any speed training at all. Due to his/her unique genetic make-up their muscle fibres may have the perfect balance already, making it possible to complete an endurance event in a good time, without the need for specific speed training.

Only you know your body and how it is responding to training – the best advice is to listen to it.

Steady Run

As it suggests, a steady run is a run within your aerobic threshold – a comfortable pace you feel you could sustain for a long period of time.

OPPOSITE: A runner enjoys a steady paced run.

In the closing stages of a long, steady run, try increasing your pace as you approach the finish. Finishing a distance run with a strong or even sprint finish will leave a positive end to your training run, leaving you confident that you finished the run on a high.

Tempo Run

A tempo-based run is run at a pace that is a stage quicker than a steady pace. A general guide to the intensity that you should be aiming for during a tempo run is that your heart rate should be around 80–85 per cent of HRM. You should be running at just below your anaerobic threshold. At this intensity, talking is just about possible but you should only be able to manage short sentences before needing to take a breath.

Tempo running is quicker than a steady run, but is not excessively fast.

The length of time that you are able to maintain a tempo-paced run varies, depending on your fitness level. Beginners may initially find that a one-mile tempo run is tough going, but a good runner may be able to maintain tempo pace for about 8 to 10 miles (13 to 16 kilometres) at least. As your fitness levels improve, you will find that tempo runs gradually become easier to maintain for longer periods as your anaerobic threshold increases.

The great thing about tempo runs is they are highly effective at preparing your body to be able to tolerate a faster paced run. If you kept your training intensity at a steady pace throughout your preparations your body would simply just adapt to that intensity and anything quicker would result in early fatigue. By overloading it in a tempo run, your heart, lungs and legs adapt to the higher intensity, not only improving your fitness levels but more importantly improving your anticipated finish time.

As tempting as it may be, try to avoid running at an intensity higher than 80–85 per cent HRM, or so that you are unable to speak any words at all during your session. A tempo run is not an all-out effort, but rather is a challenging run performed at an increased pace. Most injuries are contracted through over-training and pushing too hard for long periods, so try to keep a check on how hard you are pushing yourself.

Fartlek Training

Now we're getting to the serious side of training. This is not to say that steady runs or tempo runs should not be taken seriously, but fartlek training is regarded by many to be the toughest part of training. Equally, it brings about the greatest fitness gains.

Translated, the Swedish word 'fartlek' means 'speed play'. As its translation would suggest, fartlek sessions involve a series of

A group of runners doing a fartlek session.

uns, whereby your running pace is increased significantly for short bursts. These increases n running speed help the body to build up tolerance to the accumulation of lactic acid n the working muscles. Over time this will not only help to increase your anaerobic threshold but also help with your general running speed.

Fartlek training, as you can see, draws a similar parallel with tempo runs, the significant difference being that the runs are performed at a higher intensity and have brief rest periods. Fartlek sessions are fantastic for adding a touch of variety to a 40–60 minute run, whilst having the added benefit of boosting your fitness levels. There are no strict rules with fartlek training, so long as you add variety and keep overloading your body.

A fartlek session: Example 1

Start out on a 45 minute run at a steady pace for about 5 to 10 minutes, to warm up. Once you feel warmed up, set yourself a landmark several hundred metres away and increase your pace significantly (at, if not above, anaerobic threshold) until you reach it. Take a few minutes to recover, and then repeat the process until you have finished your run.

A fartlek session: Example 2

Start out on a 45 minute run at a steady pace for 5 minutes to warm up. Using your heart rate monitor watch or a stopwatch, significantly increase your pace to one that you can just about maintain for 2 minutes, and recover for the next 3 minutes. Repeat this process eight times to complete your 45 minute run. Such a session would be encrypted like this:

45 minutes – 5 minutes WU, then 2 minutes @ AT/LT with 3 minutes REC. Repeat 8 times.

A fartlek session: Example 3

Ideally, for this session you should know exactly when each mile has elapsed, by knowing specific landmarks or by previously marking each mile point yourself.

Set out on an 8 mile run, beginning at a steady pace. Once you have completed the first mile, increase your pace to anaerobic threshold or above for the second mile. Once you have completed your quick mile, use the third mile to recover by running at a recovery pace, at or just below a steady pace. Repeat each stage until you have finished the 8 miles/13km.

This session is tough and should only be done when you have built up a solid running base. However, the session can be fully adapted to your specific running ability. As

Cones – used to mark out distances for interval training.

long as your fast mile is run at a pace that you feel you could only just sustain for that mile, you are running at the correct intensity.

Varying fartlek sessions

To write down all of the different types of fartlek sessions you could do would take up the majority of the book. There are so many ways to vary these sessions that the best approach is to see which types of session you prefer. As long as you know the reasons why you need to include fartlek sessions in your running schedule, you are in a position to make your own up.

However, as a rough guide, the variances you need to consider to keep overloading the body are:

- Increase the circuit distance by a few miles
- Increase your running or recovery pace.
- Increase the time of the quick run by 30 seconds or a minute.
- Decrease the time of your recovery.
- Incorporate some small hills into the run.

Feel free to mix and match all of these variables for a fartlek run. So long as you are careful not to progress too quickly and you are not pushing yourself too hard, you will find your fitness levels will improve immeasurably.

Interval Training

Interval training is very similar to fartlek, the only difference being that it is generally more structured. During a fartlek session random distances can be covered with each 'fast' section, whereas with interval training you generally tend to stick with a specific distance and recovery time for a set number of running intervals. Cones are often used as distance markers, so that you know how far you have run during each interval. An example of an interval training session may involve running 400 metres eight times, with a rest period of 3 minutes between each interval.

Ideally, interval training is best performed on a running track but a park or football field are excellent alternatives. It is advisable, if you choose to run in a park or field, to ensure that the surface is fairly flat and free of large bumps or holes. Interval training is run at pace, giving you far less time to see any oncoming undulation in the ground. One foot in the wrong place can easily cause you to turn your ankle, leading to a significant amount of time off training.

As with fartlek sessions, interval sessions can be varied in a number of ways. Examples include:

- Increase the speed of the interval.
- Increase the number of intervals.
- Increase the distance of the intervals.
- Decrease recovery time.
- Include hills.

The same principles apply to interval training as they do to fartlek. Remember what you are trying to achieve. You are not trying to see how exhausted you can get during a training session by running yourself into the ground; you are running to make your heart, lungs and legs adapt to the stresses of running. By making your body adapt to a quicker pace of running, your race pace will seem a lot easier and you will be more resistant to fatigue.

If you have never attempted an interval training session before, it's a good idea to start off gently and gradually build up the intensity and number of intervals. Interval training is

Analysing heart rate during interval training.

Blood Pooling

During your rest periods, try to avoid stopping completely as this is likely to bring on a sensation of lightheadedness and disorientation, due to a condition known as blood pooling.

After an intense bout of running, the build-up of lactic acid in your legs requires a significant amount of blood to remove it and neutralize the acidity balance. By stopping moving completely, excessive amounts of blood are diverted quickly to the legs to clear the lactic acid, at the expense of your brain, giving rise to a brief episode of dizziness and disorientation. Although this is only temporary, it is fairly unpleasant and best avoided. So instead of stopping completely after your interval, keep moving around to keep the blood circulating; walking will suffice.

tough. With your heart rate likely to reach around 95 per cent of your maximum, it is advisable to start off your interval sessions with realistic targets, and as you improve you can slowly increase your session intensity.

If you have invested in a top of the range heart rate monitor, it is possible to set it so that it will beep at you when your rest period has elapsed and when you have completed the workout. The heart rate information can then be transferred to a computer and previous performances can be compared, to track any improvement.

An Interval Session: Example 1
- Find a suitable area in which to perform your training session, such as a football field, park or running track.
- Mark out a looped area of around 400 metres that is flat and free of holes. Depending on your running speed, this should take you anywhere between 50 and 80 seconds to complete at a fast pace.
- Perform a gentle warm-up with stretches for about five to ten minutes and take your place at the point you intend to start and perform the following interval session: run 400 metres eight times, with a 4 minute rest between each run.

Try to record the time it takes you to complete each interval, along with your end heart rate, using a stopwatch and/or heart rate monitor and aim to finish each one in about the same time. If you are beginning to slow down significantly in the second half of the session, you have started out too quickly and should try to run at a slightly slower pace next time.

As a guide, for the short distance intervals, you should be running each interval at about 80–90 per cent of your maximum running speed, which is just on the limit of your lactate threshold.

An Interval Session: Example 2
As with example 1, find a suitable area in which to perform the session. After a 10 minute warm-up and stretches perform the following session:

3 × 600m with 3 minutes' rest
3 × 400m with 3 minutes' rest
3 × 200m with 3 minutes' rest

Do not worry about ensuring that the distances are 100 per cent accurate, an educated guess is fine. Simply ensure that the distance you are running is around twenty to thirty seconds less each time and that you do not set out too quickly. It is so easy to set off too quickly at the beginning when you are fresh and raring to go, but it will come back to haunt you later on in the session.

Once again, if possible try to record the time it takes you to complete each interval.

An Interval Session: Example 3
Find an appropriate area to perform your training and spend a good five minutes warming up and stretching. In an ideal world, this session is best performed on a running track, but can easily be undertaken on a large field.

Try to mark out an area of about one mile (or 1.6km). This is obviously difficult to do by sight, so a bit of 'trail and error' may be needed for the first few attempts. To give you a rough guide, each interval should take about 6 to 8 minutes.

This interval session is very demanding, so be cautious when first attempting it. If you find it too easy then simply up your pace the next time.

Perform the following session:

3 × 1600m (1 mile) with a 10 minute break
   Or
3 × 6–8 mins with a 10 minute break

You are aiming to run each interval at a pace that you feel you can just about sustain for the whole distance – the last minute should begin to feel pretty uncomfortable.

As with all interval sessions, you should be aiming to complete the last interval in the same time as the first. In fact, psychologically, finishing the final run in the quickest time ends the session on a very positive note, and you will know that you have given your all to the training session.

Interval training is a remarkable tool for improving your fitness levels. After just a handful of sessions, you will not only feel a lot fitter, but your longer runs will feel so much easier. It is so important, however, that you listen to your body and avoid pushing yourself too hard.

The beauty of interval training is its adaptability. There are no strict rules. It is up to you to discover your limitations and train inside them to suit your fitness levels. Feel free to alter the examples given above in whatever way you feel best matches your fitness levels – this could mean adding or reducing the number of intervals or even increasing or decreasing your recovery time.

All you need to remember is to aim for improvement by upping the intensity once in a while – simply reducing your recovery time by 30 seconds will make a huge difference.

Interval training – some people love it, some people hate it, but everyone gets fitter from it.

Key Points
- Begin your interval sessions gently until you know your limits.
- Stop training if you have a muscle twinge or feel unwell.
- Alter the intensity, however slightly, every week or so.
- Experiment with different types and distances of interval training.
- Record your progress.
- Enjoy!

Hill Training

No matter where your race is being held, it is highly unlikely that the course will be totally flat. It is a good idea to see the profile of the course you are running, so that you can see how many inclines there are and therefore how much hill work you will need to incorporate into your training. Even if your race is as flat as a pancake, the inclusion of hill training sessions in your preparation is a fantastic way of improving your leg strength and fitness, as well as adding variety to your sessions.

By including hills into your running programme, your legs, heart and lungs have to work that much harder to combat the gravity acting against the body. The weight of gravity pushing you down makes work for the legs that much harder, which in turn causes a significant rise in heart rate, creating a far more challenging workout than a jog on the flat. Over time, hill sessions greatly increase the strength in your legs, not only adapting them for the odd incline in a race but also making running on the flat seem like a piece of cake.

There are a number of ways you can perform hill training, but a good warm-up and stretch before you train is essential. As well as being more taxing for your muscles, hills also increase stress on your tendons and ligaments, both of which you need to look after to avoid injury. Never attempt to run up a steep hill at the beginning of your run when your muscles and tendons are still not warm. Your Achilles heel is vulnerable at the best of times, especially at the beginning of a run, and even more so going up a hill at the start of a run.

There are generally three types of hill session that you can perform:

- a steady paced or tempo paced run performed over a hilly course;
- a fartlek session, using hills rather than speed to increase the intensity;

Hill training – great for the heart and legs.

- interval training – by sprinting up a hill and jogging back down.

Example of a Distance Run with Hills

The distance of this run very much depends on how far you are into your training. If you are at the beginning of your training a hilly course of a few miles is ideal, but in the latter stages of your training running for 18 miles (29km) on a hilly course should be possible.

Whichever distance you choose, the course should ideally include a number of hills of various lengths. The first time you attempt the run, it is best to be cautious and avoid running up the inclines too fast – your aim is to complete the run without stopping. During the hill climb, try to remain relaxed and maintain a balanced running rhythm. After the hill, enjoy the respite and begin to prepare yourself for the next incline.

Example of a hilly fartlek session

Choose a distance of about 5 to 7 miles or about 10 kilometres. The route should contain a number of inclines, with the start of the run as flat as possible to ensure that you are well warmed-up before tackling any hills.

The session is run just like any fartlek session, the major difference being that you 'attack' every hill that you encounter. Try to run up the hill at a pace that you feel is only sustainable for the duration of the hill. At the top of each incline, recuperate and concentrate on the next hill that awaits you.

Over time, as your body adapts to this form of training, try to increase your running speed up the hill, or include a few more hills. Whichever way you choose to increase the intensity, make sure you do it in gradual stages. Pushing yourself too hard too early is the quickest route to the physiotherapist.

Example of Interval Training on Hills

A very good warm-up is a must before you begin to attempt this session. A large amount of stress is placed on your muscles and tendons during this work-out, and it is easy to cause significant damage if they are not well warmed-up.

Choose a hill with a significant incline of around 50 to 100 metres in length. After your warm-up, sprint up the hill as fast as you can and gently jog or walk back down. The number of intervals you decide to do is entirely dependent on your fitness levels, the length of your recovery time and the length of the hill, so to provide you with a number is difficult. As always, begin modestly and build up once you realize your limits. As a rough guide, the entire workout, including the 10 minute warm-up, should last about half an hour, or if you are very fit 45 minutes.

This session is very taxing and should not be undertaken lightly. It will have a significant impact on your training, so long as you keep the sessions within your limits.

Hill training is easy to perform in principle – so long as you live near hills. Finding inclines to perform these training runs may be difficult for some people, in which case you simply have to make do with the terrain that surrounds you.

Key Points
- Due to the intense nature of hill training, it is best performed just once a week.
- Ensure you have a good warm-up to reduce the risk of injury to your muscles and tendons.
- Increase the intensity of your sessions gradually.
- If your race is set on an undulating course, be sure to incorporate plenty of hill sessions into your training.

CROSS TRAINING

The usefulness of cross training is often underestimated by runners, and is completely ignored by some. Naturally, the bulk of your training will be running but by incorporating a variety of other cardiovascular disciplines, you will not only help to break away from the monotony of running but also help to save your joints from its repetitive nature. Cross training may not necessarily help you to run quicker but in the case of an injury it could be the only thing saving you from losing your hard-earned fitness levels.

The type of cross training you choose to include in your training schedule is very much up to you. There is a wide range of activities you can do other than running that can really tax your cardiovascular system and complement your running training.

Some of the most popular forms of cross training include:

- treadmill;
- swimming;
- indoor rowing;
- cycling;
- elliptical cross trainer.

Treadmills

Although it could be argued that tread-mill sessions do not strictly come under the heading of cross training, if you are new to running it is a good idea to begin running on a treadmill. The conveyor belt helps to absorb impact, significantly reducing the amount of shock on your joints, and although your limbs will eventually learn to adapt to the various stresses that road running presents, a treadmill is fantastic not only as a way to begin training, but also used in conjunction with your marathon preparations. Running in strong winds, horizontal rainfall and black ice, some may argue, is 'character building', but less serious runners may justifiably believe that their characters are built up sufficiently and settle for a session on a treadmill instead.

Treadmills are also a fantastic way to train in the dark winter months. Many women feel unsafe running alone at night so rather than avoiding a run in the evening, a treadmill provides the perfect opportunity to ease the burden on your joints, shelter from wet and windy weather and run in a safe environment.

Swimming

Swimming is perhaps the most popular form of cross training. It is non weight-bearing, which provides the muscles and joints with a welcome rest from pounding the streets. Whether you choose to swim lengths of a pool or 'run' in the water, it is important that you put a great deal of effort into water sessions so that your heart rate is elevated and

Swimming is ideal if you are injured.

OPPOSITE: *Treadmills add variety and safety in the winter months.*

Rowing is a fantastic form of cross training.

your cardiovascular system is being taxed. Swimming gently up and down the pool as if you were on holiday may seem like the perfect form of cross training but sadly it is pointless as far as your fitness is concerned. Aim to swim at an intensity that gets you breathless, so that you leave the pool feeling as though you have had a workout.

Indoor Rowing

A rowing machine is an impact-free activity, making it a fantastic choice as an alternative to running. Rowing is a highly effective form of exercise and is thought to be one of the best overall forms of fitness training.

Although there is a variety of rowing machines available, Concept2 provide perhaps the highest quality and most inter-active machine available. Using computer graphics to help motivate you and a function that enables rowers to compete with others over the Internet, this form of cross training can be great fun.

It is advisable to get a little advice on rowing technique before you use a rowing ergometer, but once you are familiar with it, performing one row a week for thirty to forty minutes will complement your running programme perfectly. As with the swimming, you must be sure to put effort into your session. If you are using a heart rate monitor, you should be aiming for a heart rate of no less than 75 per cent MHR. You should finish your row breathless and sweaty.

Cycling

Whether you choose to cycle indoors or out on the road, cycling can help develop good leg strength and provide a very hard workout for your heart and lungs.

If you decide to take to the road, try to choose an undulating route that is going to

Cycling adds variety to your running regime.

make you work hard. Cycling on the flat is better than nothing, but with the number of gears on today's bikes life is made too easy and the temptation to cycle gently is sometimes hard to resist.

If you use an indoor bike, you have the luxury of being able to watch television and climb a hill at the same time. Vary your indoor cycling sessions by upping the resistance every now and again for a few minutes to simulate an incline.

As with the rowing machine, aim to keep your heart rate working in at least your aerobic zone, with the odd increase of intensity pushing it higher.

Elliptical Cross Trainer

Sometimes known as a Nordic Track, a cross trainer simulates a cross-country skiing action. As with an indoor bike, the resistance can be altered to simulate an incline and therefore increasing the intensity of your workout. The action is smooth and non-impact, making it a fantastic alternative to running.

Whichever form of cross training you choose, it is important that you enjoy it. If you would rather spend an hour at the dentist than an hour on an exercise bike then maybe you should consider choosing another type of exercise. Remember, as long as you are pushing yourself and your heart rate is around 75 per cent MHR, then you're training is worthwhile.

Cross Training Duration

The length of time your cross training sessions should take very much depends on your fitness levels and how far you are through your running programme. As a general rule, once you are a few weeks into your training and your fitness has reached a reasonable level, you should be aiming to be spending anywhere from 40 minutes to an hour on cross training sessions. Whether this involves the session being performed on the same machine or using three forms of cross training is very much up to you.

There may be instances, however, when cross training sessions may need to last longer. With the London Marathon being held in April, British runners find that some of their distance runs need to be undertaken in freezing conditions. In the extreme cold, ice poses a major threat to the safety of runners so embarking on an eighteen mile run with black ice underfoot is a risk that is best not taken. If access to a treadmill is not possible, an aerobic cross training session of several hours is the ideal alternative.

Cross Training with an Injury

As all runners are aware, injuries can crop up at any time during your race preparations, meaning that every once in a while training has to be put on hold for a few days or sometimes even weeks. Minor muscle and tendon strains to the lower leg are amongst the most common afflictions that runners experience, causing frustration at not being able to run. However, injury need not necessarily mean a complete cessation to training. Depending on the nature of the injury, at least one form of cross training can usually be used to maintain fitness levels and prevent the runner from becoming excessively agitated by a lack of running. Simply substituting your runs with an alternative form of exercise for similar lengths of time and intensity will prevent your fitness levels from dropping and will keep your training momentum going.

If you are unfortunate enough to pick up an injury and running is out of the question, find a form of cross training that you enjoy and, above all, does not aggravate the injury. If in doubt, it is best to seek professional advice, not only to diagnose the injury, but also to ensure that further damage cannot be done by continuing to exercise.

Key Points
- Use cross training as a complement, not a substitute, to your training unless you have an injury.
- Try to keep a heart rate of at least 75 per cent MHR during a session.
- Vary your cross training as much as you like – row, bike and swim all in one session if you want to.
- Choose a type of cross training that you enjoy. If you only like rowing, for example, then stick with it but keep the sessions challenging.

By adding variety to your training, you are not only less likely to get bored with the same weekly routine but you will encourage your body to adapt to and tolerate the stresses of marathon training far better than simply

The cross trainer is low impact and highly cardiovascular.

running long distances. This is particularly true of the speed-work sessions (intervals and fartlek) but caution must be taken to avoid excessive stress on your body. Not only can speed work sessions in themselves cause injury due to their high intensity, but coupled with long-distance runs muscle niggles can easily be contracted. You need to know early on, by listening to your body, how well you tolerate all varieties of training, and above all slowly increase weekly mileage and speed sessions to allow your body to adapt.

CHAPTER 7

The Training Part 2: The Half Marathon

Whether you are moving up from competing in 6.2 mile/10km races, taking part in your first endurance event, or using the half marathon as a stepping stone to prepare for a full marathon, a 13.1 mile (21km) run is the first distance that enters the 'endurance running' category. Whereas any reasonably fit person could make their way around a 10km course, to complete a half marathon without stopping takes weeks of preparation and it is a distance that must not be underestimated. The fact that three people lost their lives whilst competing in the BUPA Great North Run in Newcastle, England in 2005 is proof in itself that the distance is challenging and must be respected.

This chapter provides you with two separate training schedules. Which one you choose to follow very much depends on the time you anticipate running in the race. If you are unsure at this stage, do not worry. I have trained a number of beginners who start their training hoping to break the 2 hour mark, only to realize further into their training that they have the ability to finish 15 minutes quicker.

The two training plans are fully interlinking. If you begin by following the first timetable and feel like 'dipping' into the second one either permanently or every now and again that is fine. Everyone has such varying ability and aptitude when it comes to running that to a large part you are the best judge on how you are progressing with your training. If you feel that the first schedule is not taxing you enough, then you have to use your initiative and decide to move over to the more advanced timetable, with the possibility of reverting back if necessary. Above all, listen to your body and avoid trying to break the land speed record on every training run.

DISTANCE OR TIME?

While following the training timetables, not only do you have the luxury of interlinking

The BUPA Great North Run, the biggest half marathon in the UK.

the two plans but you can also vary the way you measure the length of your sessions. All training schedules you read will vary in one way or another but a major difference is whether you are advised to cover a certain distance or achieve a certain time. Ultimately, it is your choice just as long as you ensure you cover a similar distance.

For example, if your goal is a 2 hour marathon (9:09 minutes/mile pace) and the plan suggests you need to do a 10 mile run, for a change you may choose to opt for a 90 minute run instead. Provided that you still perform every run covering a known distance, you can mix and match as often as you like.

> Try varying the way you run your sessions. Why not alternate weeks – one week run by time, the next week run by distance.

THE COMPLETE NOVICE

Many training programmes for the half marathon generally draw up a 10 to 12 week training schedule. Whereas this approach may be suitable for already conditioned runners, to expect an individual new to running to go from feeling exhausted after running a short distance to catch a bus, to running 13.1 miles three months later is quite some ask. Just 12

weeks of training leaves leaving little allow ance for injuries or illness.

Before you can begin the following trainin schedule, you need to very slowly build up you fitness to be able to run 3 miles (5km). Just 30 minute session of interspersed walking an light jogging slowly begins to prepare you joints, muscles and heart for harder session in the months to come. Gradually increas these sessions in duration and intensity a your fitness levels increase but take care no to overdo it. Once you can comfortably jo 3 miles (5km) without stopping, then you ar ready to start the beginners' schedule.

If you have never run before, try followin the timetable opposite. As with the othe training schedules, feel free to adapt it b making it easier or harder, but above all d not rush. The more time you take adaptin the body to running, the less money you wi have to spend at the physiotherapists.

WHAT IS YOUR GOAL?

Before you decide which training programm to follow, you must first of all choose whicl category you think you fall into, so tha you begin following the most appropriat timetable.

As a rough guide, if you are entering you

Two runners finish the Great North Run with a smile.

3 mile/5km Walk and Run Programme

Week	Monday	Tuesday	Wednesday	Thursday	Friday	Saturday	Sunday
1	Brisk 3km walk	Rest	Brisk 1.8–2.4m/3–4km walk	Rest	Brisk 2.4km/4km walk	Rest	1min jog, 4min walk (×5)
2	Rest or light walk	Rest	1min jog, 3min walk (×5)	Rest	Brisk 3m/5km walk	Rest	1–2min jog, 4min walk (×6)
3	Rest or light walk	Rest	1–2min jog, 3min walk (×5)	Rest	1–2min jog, 3min walk (×5)	Rest	2–3min jog, 4min walk (×5)
4	Brisk walk with occasional jog	Rest	2–3min jog, 3min walk (×4)	Rest	2–3min jog, 3min walk (×4)	Rest	3–4min jog, 3min walk (×5)
5	Rest or light walk	Rest	4min jog, 2–3min walk (×6)	Rest	4min jog, 1–2min walk (×6)	Rest	5min jog, 2min walk (×5)
6	Rest or light walk	Rest	5–6min jog, 1–2min walk (×5)	Rest	6–7min jog, 2min walk (×5)	Rest	7–8min jog, 2min walk (×5)
7	Rest or light walk	Rest	8min jog, 2–3min walk (×4)	Rest	8–9min jog, 1–2min walk (×3)	Rest	9–10min jog, 2–3min walk (×4)
8	Rest or light walk	Rest	10min jog, 2–3min walk (×4)	Rest	10min jog, 2min walk (×5)	Rest	11–12min jog, 1–2min walk (×3)
9	Rest or light walk	Rest	12min jog, 1–2min walk (×2)	Rest	12min jog, 1–2min walk (×3)	Rest	13–14min jog, 2–3min walk (×2)
10	Rest or light walk	Rest	15min jog, 2–3min walk (×2)	Rest	15min jog, 2min walk (×2)	Rest	16–17min jog, 1–2min walk (×2)
11	Rest or light walk	Rest	16–17min jog, 1–2min walk (×2)	Rest	15min jog, 1 min walk (×2)	Rest	15min jog, 1min walk (×3)
12	Rest or light walk	Rest	10min jog, 1–2min break (×2)	Rest	40min walk and jog	Rest	2.4–3m/4–5km run

first half marathon and are a newcomer to the world of running, I would advise you to begin following the first programme, which is designed to help you finish in two hours plus, bearing in mind that you can incorporate sessions from the advanced schedule should you feel it necessary.

If you have already competed in a few running events or already have a good level of fitness, then the second timetable will probably be more suitable. By following the schedule in the more advanced timetable, there is no reason why you should not be able to break the elusive 1 hour, 30 minutes barrier.

The table on the right provides the split times per mile that you should follow in order to complete the race in your anticipated time. Throughout your training, it is essential that you keep tabs on your average time per mile, so that you can develop a realistic expectation of how quickly you will complete the half marathon.

Minutes per Mile Guide	
Finishing time	*Average minutes per mile/kilometre*
3hrs 00mins	13:43/8:04
2hrs 45mins	12:35/7:27
2hrs 30mins	11:26/6:50
2hrs 15mins	10.17/6:12
2hrs 00mins	9:09/5:35
1hr 45mins	8:00/4:58
1hr 30mins	6:51/4:15

Enjoyment is the main aim for beginners.

A quick race requires dedication to training.

It is important to keep your goals realistic, so that you are not setting yourself a finishing time that you are unlikely to achieve. For example, if you hope to finish the race in less than 2 hours, and 4 weeks away from race day you can only manage mile splits of over 10 minutes/mile, it is highly unlikely that you will achieve your goal. By keeping track of your mile splits and knowing your running capabilities, it will save you disappointment when you cross the finishing line. Aiming high and pushing yourself is one thing, being realistic with you goals is another.

BEGINNERS' TIMETABLE

This timetable is ideal for those wishing to finish the race in a time of anywhere between 2 to 3 hours. Keep an eye on the advanced timetable as well, as you would certainly benefit from including some harder runs if you feel up to it.

Beginners' Half Marathon Programme							
Week	**Day 1**	**Day 2**	**Day 3**	**Day 4**	**Day 5**	**Day 6**	**Day 7**
1	Gentle 3m/5km jog	Rest	3m/5km gentle fartlek	Rest	30min jog/ cross train	Rest	3–4m/5– 6.5km steady
2	Rest	Rest	3m/5km gentle fartlek	Rest	40min jog/walk	Rest	4m/6.5km steady
3	Rest	Rest	4m/6.5km gentle fartlek	Rest	3m/5km easy jog	Rest	5m/8km steady
4	Gentle 3m/ 5km or rest	Rest	30mins hills	Rest	3m/5km jog	Rest	4–5m/6.5– 8km tempo
5	Rest	Rest	30mins intervals	Rest	4m/6.5km jog	Rest	5–6m/8– 10km steady
6	3m/5km easy or rest	Rest	4m/6.5km hard fartlek	Rest	45mins cross train	Rest	6–7m/10– 11km steady
7	3m/5km easy or rest	Rest	40mins hills	Rest	3–4m/5–6.5km jog	Rest	7–8m/11– 13km steady
8	Rest or easy 3m/5km jog	Rest	40mins intervals	Rest	4m/6.5km jog	Rest	5–6m/8– 10km tempo
9	Rest	Rest	5–6m/8– 10km fartlek	Rest	50mins cross train	Rest	8–9m/13– 14.5km steady
10	Rest	Rest	40mins hills	Rest	5m/8km steady	Rest	9–10m/14.5– 16km steady
11	Rest	Rest	40mins intervals	Rest	5m/8km steady	Rest	10m/16km steady
12	Rest or easy 3m/5km	Rest	4–5m/6.5– 8km fartlek	Rest	Cross train or 5m/8km	Rest	11–12m/17.5 –19km quick
13	Rest or easy 4m/6.5km jog	Rest	40mins hills	Rest	Cross train or 4m/6.5km	Rest	12m/19km steady
14	Rest	Rest	5m/8km fartlek	Rest	Cross train or easy 4m/6.5km	Rest	12–13m/19– 21km steady
15	Rest or easy 4m/6.5km jog	Rest	4–5m/6.5–8km at race pace	Rest	Cross train or 4m/6.5km	Rest	6–8m/10–13km at race pace
16	Gentle 3m/ 5km or rest	Rest	Gentle 3m/5km	Rest	Gentle 2–3m/ 3–5km	Rest	RACE DAY

Advanced Half Marathon Programme

Week	Day 1	Day 2	Day 3	Day 4	Day 5	Day 6	Day 7
1	Gentle 4–5m/ 6.5–8km jog	Rest	45mins fartlek	Rest	4–5m/6.5–8km tempo	Rest	5–6m/8–10km steady
2	Gentle 4–5m/ 6.5–8km jog	Rest	40mins intervals	Rest	5–6m/8–10km tempo	Rest	6–7m/10–11km steady
3	Cross train/ rest	Rest	5mins fartlek	Rest	6m/10km tempo	Rest	7–8m/11–13km steady
4	Rest or easy 4m/6.5km jog	Rest	5mins fartlek	Rest	5m/8km steady	Rest	6m/10k fast
5	Cross train/ rest	Rest	45mins intervals	Rest	5m/8km tempo	Rest	8–9m/13–14.5km steady
6	Cross train/ rest	Rest	40mins hills	Rest	60mins cross train	Rest	10–11m/16–17.5km quick
7	Cross train/ rest	Rest	45mins intervals	Rest	6m/10km tempo	Rest	11–12m/17.5–19km steady
8	Rest/easy 4m/6.5km jog	Rest	5–6 miles fartlek	Rest	4–5m/6.5–8km tempo	Rest	13–14m/21–22.5km steady
9	Rest/easy 4m/6.5km jog	Rest	40mins intervals	Rest	5–6m/8–10km tempo	Rest	8–10m/13–16km steady
10	Rest/easy 3m/5km jog	Rest	easy 5 mile jog	Rest	3–4m/5–6.5km jog	Rest	RACE DAY

Key Points on How to Use the Beginners' Timetable

• Remember that it is just a guide, you do not necessarily have to follow it word for word.
Never run if you are carrying an injury; it will only make it worse. If an injury persists, seek professional advice.

• Do not be afraid of looking at the advanced schedule and incorporate some sessions if you feel up to it.
• Do not feel guilty if you miss the odd run. Life has a pleasant or sometimes unpleasant habit of getting in the way of training. If you miss a couple weeks of training, go back a week or so in the timetable and build your fitness levels back up again.

ADVANCED TIMETABLE

If you are a regular runner or already have a good level of fitness, then the advanced training schedule should build your running fitness up to be able to break both the 2 hour and the 90 minute barriers. However, if your goal is to finish the half marathon in around the 90 minute mark or quicker, you may benefit from including one or two extra runs per week. If you are a natural runner, adding extra runs may not be necessary, but keep a constant eye on your progress and note how comfortable you feel meeting your mile splits on long runs. If you are struggling, an extra fartlek session every few weeks or so may be just the ticket to boost your fitness.

The 10-week plan is designed to provide realistic training sessions for busy people who may not have the time to train 5 days a week. This has the added benefit of preventing over-training and the risk of contracting an

---

If you have aspirations to run much quicker than 90 minutes, it is worth seeking alternative training sessions to use in conjunction with this one.

---

injury. However, if you have the time available and sense not to push yourself too hard, there is no reason why you cannot add an extra session or two in per week.

Key Points on How to Use the Advanced Timetable

- Never be tempted to run with an injury.
- If you wish to include extra sessions never attempt to do fartlek, interval or hill sessions on consecutive days. These are high intensity sessions and the body needs time to rest and recover.
- Feel free to alter the odd session every now and again. So if you feel like doing a 45 minute fartlek instead of a 45 minute hill session, go for it.
- On your long runs, keep a regular check that your minutes per mile pace is consistent with your anticipated finishing time. If you are finding the pace tough going, either up your training or change your goal – there's always next year.

For information on how to run the race itself and things to remember on race day, refer to Chapter 14.

CHAPTER 8

The Training Part 3: The Marathon

Although it is not advisable, some people reading this book may have decided to jump straight in at the deep end and go from never having run before to entering a full marathon.

That is not to say that the task is impossible, but runners must be aware of the hard work that lies ahead. Ideally, you should slowly build up your mileage over several months, especially if you are a new runner, but provided you are sensible there is no reason why you cannot attempt the 26.2 miles.

The two timetables that follow are designed on the assumption that you are able to run 4 to 5 miles (6 to 8km), so if you are not yet at this level it is advisable not to begin either programme until you have reached this level of fitness.

Although it is a cliché, the marathon distance should be respected. If you intend to compete in a marathon you should do so with the intention of running it. First and foremost, the marathon is a running event, which is one of the main reasons why people are respected so much for completing it. Marathon finishers are not only admired for finishing the distance but also for the months of hard training that goes into preparing the body to run it. Naturally, in some cases such as severe dehydration or low blood sugar, stopping running is necessary for health reasons, but your race preparations should be comprehensive enough to avoid such problems. As soon as the gun is fired and the race is under way, you should have the intention of running until you cross the finishing line. You know you will be tired in the latter stages of the race, but unless you feel dizzy or unwell you should fight every desire to walk – you will only regret it later if you do.

The following training plans, like the ones for the half marathon, are split into two. The first plan is aimed at the slower or first-time marathon runners and should allow you to finish the race in 4^1/$_2$ to 5^1/$_2$ hours. The second plan is tougher, and if followed correctly should allow you to break the 4 and the 3^1/$_2$ hour barrier.

WHAT IS YOUR GOAL?

As with the half marathon, before you know which plan to follow you need to have some kind of an idea of how quickly you want to run the race. If you have no idea, begin by following the first plan and see how your training goes. By noting your mile splits on a long run, using the table below, you will soon be able get an idea as to the time you think is feasible.

Throughout your training, it is essential that you keep tabs on your average time per mile, so that you can develop a realistic expectation on how quickly you will complete race.

Remember to keep your goals realistic and do not fall into the trap of thinking that come race day adrenalin will help you run your mile splits ten seconds faster. There is no doubt that many people perform better on race day, but setting yourself an unrealistic goal usually results in disappointment.

The London Marathon – one of the most popular in the world.

Minutes per Mile Guide	
Finishing time	*Average minutes per mile/km*
3hrs 00mins	6:52/4:15
3hrs 15mins	7:26/4:37
3hrs 30mins	8:00/4:58
4hrs 00mins	9:09/5:35
4hrs 15mins	9:43/6:02
4hrs 30mins	10:17/6:12
5hrs 00mins	11:26/6:50
5hrs 15mins	12:00/7:28
5hrs 30mins	12:35/7:49
6hrs 00mins	13:43/8:32

Estimating Your Marathon Time Using Your Half Marathon Time

As part of your marathon training, it is strongly recommended that you compete in at least one half marathon event. This will not only give you first hand experience of the excitement, nerves and atmosphere you are likely to experience come the big day, but some running experts believe that you can estimate your marathon time by comparing it to your half marathon time. For example:

Half Marathon	Marathon
2:00	4:30
1:45	4:00
1:30	3:15
1:15	2:45

These estimates are a fantastic guide but do not take them as a given. Just because you have just run a 1:45 half marathon, it does not guarantee that you will finish the marathon in

4 hours; it merely suggests that you have the physiological capability to do it. There are so many more factors that come into play in the full marathon that you can take nothing for granted. Heat, dehydration, insufficient distance training, other runners and injury are just a few of the pitfalls you have to avoid if you want to prove the accuracy of the prediction tables.

TAPERING

The term 'tapering' often confuses new marathon runners, and is not generally understood. Put simply, tapering is the gradual reduction of training intensity and duration as you get closer to race day. It is a necessary aspect of endurance training and it starts in the last few weeks before the big day.

Your last big run should be around three weeks before the race; after that, the body needs to be given time to recover and repair itself before it is faced with the full 26.2 miles (42.2km). This is not to say that you should stop training altogether, put your feet up and watch television, but the tapering period should be a gradual reduction in running.

Tapering is often an incredibly frustrating time for runners. You have spent the past three or so months training hard and the reduction in training can make some people feel like a caged animal. During the three week tapering period, it is common for people to think that, despite all the hard training, they are still not fit enough and they are often tempted to embark on a handful of hard sessions to top up their fitness levels. Don't do it. If you aren't fit enough before you begin your training wind-down, a few more hard training sessions are not going to make any significant difference and the risk you run of picking up an injury is not worth it.

Most of you reading this will completely ignore the advice, because most people do, but please do try to resist the temptation to do more than you have to. You will not lose

Finishing with a smile.

your fitness during the tapering period. In fact, if you do it properly you are likely to feel fresher on race day than you have ever felt.

BEGINNERS' TIMETABLE

This timetable assumes that your main goal is the marathon, not the half marathon. As a result, the 16 week plan starts out from the beginning and assumes that you can complete a 5 mile (8km) jog without stopping.

In an ideal world, a marathon training plan for a fairly new runner should be much longer than 16 weeks, to ensure the body is slowly adapted to the increasing running distances. However, for many people to commit themselves to a training plan of longer than 4 months is a big ask. If you have the luxury of time at your disposal and do not mind preparing your body a little slower for the race, then I would strongly advise you to repeat one week every 3 or 4 weeks, so that your legs have that much more time to adapt to the rigours of training.

The following timetable is ideal for the first time marathon runner and busy people who may not be able to run more than three or four times a week. The schedule is designed to be started 16 weeks before your race.

Key Points on How to Use the Beginners' Timetable

- Remember that it is just a guide, you do not necessarily have to follow it word for word.
- Never run if you are carrying an injury, it'll only make it worse. If an injury persists, seek professional advice.
- Don't be afraid of looking at the advanced schedule and incorporate some sessions if you feel up to it.
- Don't feel guilty if you miss the odd run. Life has a pleasant or sometimes unpleasant habit of getting in the way of training. If you miss a week or two of training, however, go back a week or so in the timetable and build your fitness levels back up again.

WEEK	Day 1	Day 2	Day 3	Day 4	Day 5	Day 6	Day 7
			Beginner's Marathon Programme				
1	Gentle 3-4m/ 5–6.5km jog	Rest	Gentle 4m/ 6.5km fartlek	Rest	30min walk/ jog	Rest	5–6m/8– 10km steady
2	Gentle 3m/5km jog	Rest	4m/6.5km fartlek or jog	Rest	40min jog/ walk	Rest	5–6m/8– 10km steady
3	Rest	Rest	4m/6.5km fartlek	Rest	5m/8km steady	Rest	6–7m/10– 11km steady
4	Gentle 3m/ 5km or rest	Rest	30mins hills	Rest	3m/5km steady	Rest	6–7m/10– 11km steady
5	Gentle 3m/ 5km or rest	Rest	4m/6.5km fartlek	Rest	4m/6.5km steady	Rest	5m/8km tempo
6	Rest	Rest	30mins hills	Rest	Cross train	Rest	7–8m/11– 13km steady
7	Rest	Rest	45–60mins cross train	Rest	45mins fartlek	Rest	8m/13km steady
8	Rest/easy 3m/5km jog	Rest	4m/6.5km jog quickly	Rest	5m/8km jog	Rest	8–10m/13– 16km steady
9	Rest/easy 3m/5km jog	Rest	30–40mins intervals	Rest	4m/6.5km jog	Rest	10–12m/ 16– 19km steady
10	Rest/easy 4m/ 6.5km steady	rest	45mins hills	Rest	4m/6.5km jog	Rest	13–14m/ 21–22.5km steady
11	Rest	Rest	6m/10km tempo	Rest	45mins hills	Rest	14–16m/ 22.5–25.5km steady
12	Rest/easy 4m/ 6.5km steady	Rest	60mins fartlek	Rest	cross train or 6m/10km	Rest	16–18m/ 25.5–29km steady
13	Rest/easy 4m/ 6.5km steady	Rest	40mins intervals	Rest	cross train or 6m/10km	Rest	18-20m/ 29– 32km steady
14	Rest	Rest	4–5m/6.5– 8km fartlek	Rest	cross train or 6m/10km	Rest	10m/16km tempo
15	Rest/easy 4m/ 6.5km steady	Rest	5–6m/8– 10km tempo	Rest	cross train or 6m/10km	Rest	6m/8km at race pace
16	Gentle 3m/ 5km or rest	Rest	Gentle 2– 3m/3–5km	Rest	Gentle 2– 3m/3–5km	Rest	RACE DAY

RbK
30
Reebok Bristol
Half Marathon 2006
www.bristolhalfmarathon.com

			Advanced Marathon Programme				
WEEK	**Day 1**	**Day 2**	**Day 3**	**Day 4**	**Day 5**	**Day 6**	**Day 7**
1	Gentle 5m/ 8km jog	45mins fartlek	4m/6.5km easy jog	Rest	Cross train/ 5m/8km jog	Rest	6–7m/ 10–11km steady
2	Gentle 4–5m/ 6.5–8km Jog	45mins fartlek	5m/8km easyjog	40min cross train	45 min intervals	Rest	7–8m/ 11–13km
3	Cross train/rest	60mins hills	Rest or 4m/6.5km easy	8m/13km steady	45mins fartlek	Rest	7–8m/ 11–13km tempo
4	Gentle 30min jog	40mins intervals	Rest or 5m/8km easy	40mins hills	45mins cross train	Rest	6m/10km fast
5	Cross train/rest	45mins fartlek	Rest or 4m/6.5km easy	45mins hills	4m/6.5km steady/ cross train	Rest	8–10m/ 13–16km steady
6	Cross train/rest	30mins hill sprints	Rest or 5m/8km easy	8m/13km fartlek	5m/8km steady	Rest	8–10m/ 13–16km tempo
7	5m/8km steady	60mins fartlek	Rest or 4m/6.5km easy	6m/10km tempo	60mins cross train	Rest	13m/ 21km steady
8	Rest or easy 5m/8km	45mins fartlek	Rest or 4m/6.5km easy	45mins intervals	90mins cross train	Rest	13–14m/ 21–22.5km steady
9	Rest or easy 4m/6.5km	45mins hills	Rest or 5m/8km easy	9–10m/ 14.5–16km fartlek	Rest/cross train	Rest	15m/ 24km steady
10	Rest or easy 4m/6.5km	60mins fartlek	Rest or 5m/8km easy	45 mins hills	4m/6.5km steady	Rest	16–17m/ 25.5–27km steady
11	Rest or easy 4m/6.5km	6–8m/ 10–13km tempo	Rest	8m/13km fartlek	Rest/cross train	Rest	18m/ 29km steady
12	Rest or easy 4m/6.5km	60mins cross train/6m/ 10km	Rest	45mins intervals	Rest/cross train	Rest	18m/29km at marathon pace

OPPOSITE: *To run fast you need 100 per cent commitment.*

		Advanced Marathon Programme *continued*					
WEEK	Day 1	Day 2	Day 3	Day 4	Day 5	Day 6	Day 7
13	Rest or easy 4m/6.5km	60mins cross train/ 6m/10km	Rest	8m/13km fartlek	Rest	Rest	20–22m/ 32–35.5km steady
14	Rest	6m/10km steady	Rest	12x400m intervals	Rest	Rest	17–18m/ 27–29km steady
15	Rest or easy 4m/6.5km	6m/10km at race pace	Rest	Cross train or 6m/10km	Rest	Rest	10m/ 16km at marathon pace
16	Gentle 3m/5km or rest	Gentle 4–5m/ 6.5–8km	Rest	Gentle 3m/5km/ rest	Rest	Rest	RACE DAY

ADVANCED TIMETABLE

Everyone who finishes a marathon receives a great deal of admiration from their peers for finishing a truly gruelling event, but those who break the 4 hour and 3$\frac{1}{2}$ hour barriers receive a little more respect.

It is those barriers that the following time-table aims to get you over. Your first few weeks of training will indicate which time is most likely, so be sure to keep a close eye on the minutes per mile split table. To break 4 hours you will need to complete each mile in just under 9:09 minutes, and to finish in less than 3$\frac{1}{2}$ hours you will have to complete each mile in just about 8 minutes.

Do not underestimate the dedication required to break these barriers. You can very easily become obsessed with reaching your goal and lose sight of sensible training practices. Remember to keep a close eye on your mile splits on your long runs and ensure that you can complete each mile on split, and do so feeling comfortable and with relative ease. Running your required splits over 8 miles (13km) is one thing, doing it for 26 is another.

As with all the other training plans, if you have time on your side feel free to include one or two extra sessions per week to really give yourself the best chance to meet your goal.

Key Points on How to Use the Advanced Timetable

- Never be tempted to run with an injury.
- If you wish to include extra sessions never attempt to do fartlek, interval or hill sessions on consecutive days. These are high-intensity sessions and the body needs time to rest and recover.
- Feel free to alter the odd session every now and again. So if you feel like doing a 45 minute fartlek instead of a 45 minute hill session, go for it.
- Keep a regular check on your long runs that your minutes/mile pace is consistent with your anticipated finishing time. If you are finding the pace tough going, either up your training or change your goal – there's always next year.

For information on how to run the race itself and things to remember on race day, refer to Chapter 14.

CHAPTER 9

Staying Motivated

Once the novelty of undertaking a very specific training regime has worn off, there are going to be times when you wonder what on earth you have undertaken. As the mileage begins to creep up and the weather begins to turn nasty, training can quickly change from being an enjoyable experience to one that you dread.

The highs and lows throughout your training are all part of the 'endurance running' experience and it is important to know that at some stage the pressure of training will feel like it's getting the better of you. All it takes is the alarm clock going off at 6am, a grey, rainy day, the prospect of a 16 mile run and a minor niggle in your knee to make you wonder whether you want to continue with your training.

Lulls in motivation are not uncommon, but quitting the challenge is always an option you will live to regret. If the demands of training are getting on top of you, try following a few of the following tips to get you back on track.

REMEMBER THE REASON YOU ARE RUNNING

Whether you are running a half or full marathon, the chances are that you will be running for a charity. Spare a thought for the invaluable use the money you raise could be put to by your chosen charity. By dropping out, just because the going gets tough, you will be depriving your charity of much needed funds. Remember that even though the training is tough, at least you have the physical ability to be able to run – many people don't.

FIND INSPIRATION

We all have an inspirational figure we look up to and not necessarily in the running world. When the going gets tough, bear in mind your inspirational figure or read their book. What would they do in your situation? How would they deal with a lull in motivation? Whether your inspiration is Lance Armstrong, Margaret Thatcher, Mohammed Ali or Roger Bannister, think about what they would say to you to keep you going. Would they tell you to quit?

SEE WHAT YOU'VE ALREADY ACHIEVED

Dips in motivation tend to arise once the mileage begins to creep up and you can easily begin to feel daunted by the training that faces you and the training that lies ahead. When times get tough, try looking at what you have already achieved and how far you have come since training began. Chances are that you will look back and be pleasantly surprised at what you have already achieved. Think about what a shame it would be to throw it all in weeks before the end.

THE CONSEQUENCES OF QUITTING

It goes without saying that sometimes it may be necessary to pull out of a race through injury, but at other times when the going gets tough the prospect of quitting seems like the

most logical idea. However, have you thought about the consequences that quitting will have? You will not only let your charity down but you will have to live with the knowledge that you had a chance to complete an endurance event but decided to drop out. Lance Armstrong, the legendary American cyclist, has perhaps the best opinion on quitting. He was quoted as saying 'Pain is temporary, quitting is forever.' Think about it on your next long run.

REWARD YOURSELF

We are all just big kids at heart and our desire for treats and rewards is always there in our subconscious, so why deny yourself a treat just because you are an adult? At times of low motivation, book yourself into a health spa, or have a weekend away. Knowing that you are working towards a treat will help to motivate you to keep going and you will really feel like you have deserved that indulgence.

ATTEND A RUNNING EVENT

If you are lucky enough to live near an upcoming running event that you have not entered yourself, why not take a trip down to the finishing line and see the faces of elated runners as they cross the line? Keep in mind that in a few weeks you will be wearing a similar smile on your face as you cross the finishing line with a huge sense of accomplishment.

RUNNING FORUMS

Joining a running forum on the Internet is a great way to share your motivation issues with fellow runners. Some may even be competing in the same event as you and be in exactly the same state of mind. You will find comfort in the knowledge that you are not alone and that many other runners are going through the same experience. By using other runners as a 'sounding board' it will help to offload your worries and help you get back your motivation. Two examples of a runner's forum can be found at www.runnersworld.co.uk and www.runnersworld.com.

VARIETY

Incorporating changes into your weekly schedule can help greatly in pulling you out of a motivation lull. Even small changes such as reversing the direction in which you run your usual route can help to break up training monotony. Try visiting a friend a few miles away or in a different town, and go for a run in their area. This will provide a change of scenery and add variety to your programme, along with the possibility of enjoying a 'post run' beer with a friend.

PUT IT ALL IN PERSPECTIVE

Although it may not seem like it at times, the weeks you spend training will be over before you know it. In years to come, you will have forgotten about the hours and miles you put into your legs to prepare for the race but the resounding memory of crossing the finishing line will stay with you forever. When you feel overwhelmed by the training demands, remind yourself that in the grand scheme of things a few weeks left of training is nothing compared to the memories you will have for life of finishing an endurance event.

OPPOSITE: When the going gets tough, try to stay positive.

CHAPTER 10

Nutrition for Running

In 1809 a gentleman named Captain Barclay Allardyce performed a number of impressive feats, but perhaps his finest was walking 1,000 miles in 1,000 hours. The account of his achievement is interesting in a number of ways, but the description of his diet would make many of today's nutritionists fall off their chairs. The captain's daily diet consisted of:

Breakfast: roast chicken and a pint of beer followed by tea with bread and butter.
Lunch: steak or mutton chops washed down with more beer and a couple of glasses of wine.
Dinner: cold chicken.

The importance of good nutrition cannot be over-stated.

Captain Allardyce also provided a number of other tips for his version of 'optimum sport nutrition'. Among these were that vegetables should be avoided due to their water composition, and fish should also be avoided. Biscuits and stale bread are the only 'vegetable' matter permitted and liquids must be avoided as much as possible.

Today, Captain Allardyce's nutritional advice would be laughed at by the layman, let alone a qualified nutritionist, but it shows just how much the theories on nutrition for exercise have changed over the years. Clearly one aspect of liquid nutrition that has not changed a great deal is man's love for beer!

Advances in science and research over the years have helped sports scientists and nutritionists gain a greater understanding into the physiology of the running human body and the best ways to fuel it to perform at an optimum level. The role of biochemical individuality is once again a factor in that what works for one person may not necessarily work for another, but science has uncovered a number of fundamental facts that are relevant to all runners.

The following chapter will outline the basic principles on how to fuel your body to tolerate the demands of training and the race itself. The importance of adequate fuel intake and hydration must not be underestimated. No matter how well your 16-week training programme has gone, if you line up at the start without following the correct nutritional guidelines your race is pretty much over before you've started. You wouldn't set off

ry to avoid foods igh in fat.

The way we tolerate and utilize food varies greatly from person to person. The saying, 'One man's meat is another man's poison' could not be more apt in many aspects of sports nutrition.

n a car journey without oil and fuel, so why o it to your body?

Every year at every race, many runners nake the same mistake with their fluid intake, ad timing of carbohydrate consumption nd, worst of all, copy what a fellow runner ats. It is so important that you find out arly on in your training which foods agree vith you and which foods don't, so that you now from the start which foods you can olerate.

The three types of food that form our iet are known as the macro nutrients, more ommonly known as:

* carbohydrate;
* protein;
* fat.

During exercise the body uses all the macro nutrients to fuel the body's energy demands ut the ratio at which they are used depends n a number of factors. These factors include he speed you are going, how far you have un and of course your individuality.

Fat

At 9 calories per gram, fat is the most condensed form of energy you can eat, and is stored in the body in abundance. Even a lean human being has enough fat to supply suffi-cient energy to run over five marathons. It is such a vital source of energy that the body is keen to store it just in case it is needed in times of starvation.

Fat is the body's preferred fuel source in activities of low intensity such as sitting, sleeping, walking slowly, etc. As long as the need for energy is not required quickly, fat is used to provide the energy, with a little help from protein and carbohydrate.

Unfortunately, as energy requirements increase for activities such as running, the ratio alters from fat being the main energy provider, to the more easily utilized energy source of carbohydrate.

Good Fat and Bad Fat

Not all fat is the same. Despite the bad press that fatty foods receive, certain types of fat are in fact vital for good health and must there-fore be included in an endurance runner's diet. Believe it or not fat does have a number of health benefits. For example, without fat we would be unable to store and utilize the fat-soluble vitamins A, D, E, F and K, which are essential for everyday bodily functions such as vision, calcium absorption and blood clotting. The different types of fat that we eat come under two categories – *saturated* fat and *unsaturated* fat (mono- and polyunsaturated).

Saturated fat is 'bad fat', and is also the type of fat that dominates a western diet. It is found in all animal products and is easily identifiable as it is solid at room temperature. Although it helps to keep us insulated and is necessary to provide protection for our vital organs, it is generally acknowledged that a diet high in saturated fat leads to obesity, heart disease and hundreds of thousands of premature deaths every year.

Although avoiding saturated fat completely is virtually impossible, it is important to try to minimize the amount you eat. Put simply, consuming excess saturated fat leads to an increase in total body fat, making you heavier, and making running long distances that much more difficult.

Monounsaturated fats are in products such as olives, nuts, seeds and avocados and can be in small quantities. Olive oil is perhaps the best known type of monounsaturated fat and its health benefits are widely accepted, due to its positive effect on cholesterol. Monounsaturated fats have the ability to help

to lower the bad form of cholesterol (LDL providing major health benefits to everyone Cold pressed extra virgin olive oil drizzle over a salad is not only delicious but incredibly good for you. For the runner, an intak of moderate amounts of monounsaturate fat is acceptable, but care must be taken tha you don't overdo it. It is still fat.

Polyunsaturated fats are slightly mor complicated, but they provide us with number of health benefits. Polyunsaturate fats provide us with two types of essential fatt acids that cannot be made by the body an must therefore be provided in the diet. Th essential fatty acids of Omega 3 (fish oils an flax/linseed) and Omega 6 (vegetable oi should certainly feature in the diet of a runne due to their ability to produce hormone-lik substances known as prostaglandins.

The production of prostaglandins provide the body with a number of essential phys ological functions. The main functions o prostaglandins are to:

- regulate the release of insulin;
- regulate moods;
- regulate cholesterol levels;
- help reduce inflammation;
- help the immune system from over-reacting;
- maintain water balance;
- regulate the metabolism.

The function of prostaglandins is comple. but as can be seen from the list many rol that prostaglandins play in the body are essen tial to the runner if optimum performance to be achieved.

Key Points About Fat in the Runner's Diet

- Try to limit your intake of saturated fat.
- Eat oily fish such as salmon, herring o mackerel twice a week.

Tips to Avoid Eating Excess Saturated Fat

- Trim any excess fat off meat products such as lamb, pork and beef steaks.
- Avoid eating the skin of poultry and game.
- Limit red meat consumption to a maximum of twice a week.
- Avoid as far as possible high fat meat, fried and dairy products such as sausages, bacon, burgers, cheese, French fries, mayonnaise, butter, cream and ice cream.
- Drain away excess fat from cooked meats such as minced beef.
- Avoid fast food restaurants.
- Grill foods instead of frying them.

Chicken is a lean source of protein.

Consume olive oil from the bottle, rather than frying foods in it.

Supplement your diet with pre-prepared essential oil products. Always seek professional advice beforehand.

Get into the habit of reading food labels to see if a food has a high fat content.

PROTEIN

In the world of sports nutrition, protein is usually more closely associated with body building than long distance running, but its importance to endurance runners is certainly no less significant. The fact that the word protein means 'of primary importance' clearly indicates just how important it is.

The intake of sufficient amounts of protein is important not only as an auxiliary fuel source to be used alongside fat and carbohydrate, but also to help rebuild muscle fibres after training runs to aid the adaptation process.

Amino Acids – the Building Blocks

Proteins are made up of long chains of amino acids. Their specific structure and order determines what kind of protein they are. There are a total of around twenty-two amino acids, some of which can be made by the body when necessary (non-essential amino acids) and others that must be consumed through the diet (essential amino acids).

If essential amino acids are left out of the diet, ill health can set in and running performance can be severely impaired. By eating a well-balanced carnivorous diet, the chances of becoming deficient in the essential amino acids are unlikely as all meat products contain sufficient amounts. Such types of food are known as complete proteins. Other types of complete protein from non-animal products include quinoa and soya.

Incomplete proteins are all other types of food that do not contain all of the essential amino acids. These include vegetable, fruit and grain products. As a result, vegetarian runners should pay particularly close attention to their diet so that they are not deficient in certain amino acids. A well-balanced vegetarian diet, with a wide variety of food products, should ensure adequate amounts of all the essential amino acids.

Before protein can be used by the body to carry out everyday physiological functions and regenerate muscle tissue, it must first be

*Eggs are a quick and easy
source of protein.*

broken down by enzymes known as peptides into individual amino acids. The absence of just one amino acid can have a major impact on running performance, leaving you feeling fatigued and lack lustre. As a result, it is essential that you make sure your protein intake is not only sufficient but of good quality.

Good Bricks Build a Good Body
You'd be forgiven for believing that from the moment you are born the genes that make you who you are remain unchanged, and, irrespective of what you eat, they cannot be altered. To a degree this may be so but in fact genes are a product of protein and are replaced regularly. Your blood, enzymes, and even the structure of your genes are made by the protein you have eaten in your diet over the past six months. If the sources of protein in your diet have been of poor quality, you will have built a poor quality body that is not going to find it easy to endure a long distance running event. Your muscles and tendons could potentially cause you problems if they have been made from a poor source of protein.

To ensure you are providing your body with the best quality 'building blocks', try to make sure that the protein in your diet is of high quality, rather than the cheap processed meats you will find in products such as micro-wave meals and fast food restaurants. Lean cuts of meat from good sources and organic meats may be more expensive but the quality of your health will be far superior.

How Much Protein?

There are many theories on the optimum amount of protein a runner needs to consume if they are to meet the body's demands. Although there is a large middle ground, too little protein will hinder adequate recovery of the working muscles, and if the body takes in more protein than it can utilize it is broken down into waste products by the liver.

Whichever book you read about protein requirements for endurance runners you can be sure that you will find a range of suggestions, but if you aim to consume somewhere in the region of 1.7g of protein per kilogram of bodyweight per day, you will not go far wrong.

CARBOHYDRATES (CHO)

No matter how little you know about sports nutrition, one type of food that you are bound to have heard plenty about is the macronutrient carbohydrate. Over the years, so much attention has been given to carbohydrate rich foods both in sports nutrition and general health nutrition that many people are left confused as to whether they are beneficial or detrimental to our health. Dr Atkins created

Types of Carbohydrate	
Type	*Food examples*
Polysaccharides (complex CHO)	Bread, pasta, rice, cous cous, potatoes, noodles, beans, pulses
Monosaccharides and disaccharides	Table sugar, glucose syrup, treacle, honey, sweets, chocolate, sports drinks

sea of controversy with his world famous
et, advising dieters to severely restrict their
take of carbohydrates to lose weight.

This nutritional approach has been strongly
iticized by the majority of physicians and
llowing such a diet for an endurance event
ould leave you in a heap after the first few
iles of the race. To understand why, a little
ore must be understood about how the
ody uses carbohydrate as a fuel.

arbohydrate in the Body

he brain is arguably the most important
gan in the body and requires a steady
pply of fuel to keep it alive and functioning
ptimally. The simplest form of carbohy-
ate, glucose, keeps the brain functioning
d without it a number of health conditions
n arise. This is not an excuse to go straight
r sugary foods; your body is much smarter
an that.

Once eaten, the more complex carbohy-
ates such as rice, pasta and potatoes, are
oken down into monosaccharides with the
lp of digestive enzymes, so the body can

transport them in the blood to be utilized.
The body's internal regulation system automatically directs sugar to the areas where
it is needed, such as the brain or working
muscles.

So that we don't need to keep eating
carbohydrates every hour of the day to meet
demand, the body stores carbohydrate away
in our muscles and liver in the form of a
substance known as glycogen.

During your training and the race itself,
you are reliant on you body's internal
glycogen store to keep your legs moving.
Without a sufficient amount of glycogen,
your race or training run will slowly grind to
a halt. Although protein and fat stores can be
used to fuel movement, they are much more
difficult to break down and utilize as a fast
source of energy.

The Importance of Glycogen

The human body can store somewhere in the
region of 500g (1.1lb) of carbohydrate in the
form of glycogen, 100g of which is stored
in the liver and 400g in the muscles. These

read – an easily
epared form of
rbohydrate.

A runner hitting the wall.

stores are enough to take you to about mile 18 (29 kilometres) of the marathon.

This is the point where people say they hit the dreaded wall, because without sufficient glycogen a quick energy source is unavailable, causing the body to turn to alternative stores of energy such as fat and protein to keep movement sustained. The process of converting fat and protein into quick energy is complex and the body is unable to do it quickly enough to meet energy demands, ultimately leading to deterioration in performance.

If carbohydrate stores remain low, an insuf ficient supply of sugar is available to keep th brain working properly, giving rise to symp toms of dizziness and confusion. If exercis is continued with these symptoms, a runner' health can very quickly deteriorate causing th athlete to collapse and fall very ill. This dro in blood sugar is known as hypoglycaemi and is explained in more detail later.

Glycogen is important for any enduranc event, but it is in the marathon where it is o utmost importance. During a half maratho race, it is unlikely that you will deplete all o our glycogen stores as your liver and muscles are able to provide enough to see out the 13.1 mile (21km) race. It is still important, however, to ensure you have eaten correctly in the days running up to the race. If your glycogen stores are not filled sufficiently before the race, your pace may begin to slow towards the end as you begin to run out of energy and your blood sugar begins to drop.

Timing Carbohydrate Intake

Ensuring that you have sufficient carbohydrate to train and race effectively is not quite as simple as you may think. Unlike refuelling a car, the timing of your carbohydrate intake is vital, due to the role of enzymes in the body.

Immediately after exercise, the body secretes large amounts of an enzyme called glycogenase, making the muscles and liver highly receptive to absorbing and storing carbohydrate. The level of glycogenase in the blood is raised for about two hours, with this time frame being the optimum window for the lost carbohydrate stores to be replaced. Numerous studies have been performed on this subject and the evidence is overwhelming in favour of consuming a carbohydrate-rich meal or drink soon after a training run. If insufficient carbohydrate is eaten and the timing is wrong, performance can be severely compromised in subsequent training runs, often leaving runners confused as to why they feel so tired.

How Much Carbohydrate?

A common mistake many new endurance runners make is to believe that because they are exercising more than they ever have done before they can get away with eating much more than usual, thinking that it is necessary to do so because they are in training.

Whereas it may be true that a runner's diet needs to be richer in carbohydrate than the average person's, eating large quantities of carbohydrate-rich snacks such as doughnuts, biscuits, cake and chocolate can be counter-productive. Naturally, your calorific intake will need to increase as you progress through your training programme but it is important not to lose sight of the fact that many carbohydrate snacks are also high in saturated fat. Before you know it, you could easily end up consuming more calories than you are expending.

The most effective way to ensure you are eating sufficient amounts of carbohydrate is to concentrate on eating the complex carbohydrates such as wholemeal bread, rice, pasta and potatoes. Initially, try measuring out your food so that you get an idea as to the quantity of carbohydrate needed to meet

Daily Carbohydrate Requirements of Athletes				
Body weight	Training hours			
	1	2	3	4
7st 12lb (50kg)	200	300	400	500
9st 6lb (60kg)	300	400	500	600
11st (70kg)	400	500	600	700
12st 8lb (80kg)	500	600	700	800
14st 2lb (90kg)	600	700	800	900
15st 10lb (100kg)	700	800	900	1,000
17st 4lb (110kg)	800	900	1,000	1,100

(Adapted with the kind permission of Michael Colgan from his book Optimum Sports Nutrition. Figures are grammes.)

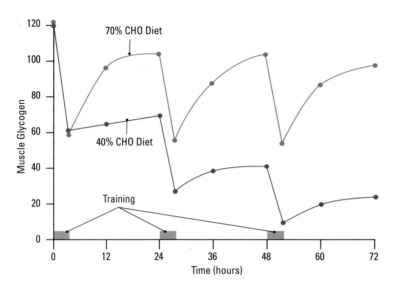

Replacement of muscle glycogen after prolonged daily training sessions.

SOURCE: D. L. Costill and J. M. Miller; *International Journal of Sports Medicine* 1:2-14 (1980)

your training demands – it may surprise you. One of the world's leading sports nutritionists, Dr Michael Colgan, devised the table on the previous page to estimate the daily carbohydrate (in grams) requirements of athletes.

This is of course a general guide and may not suit every runner's biochemistry. If you find you are putting weight on after a few weeks of training, it may be a good idea to revise your carbohydrate intake and perhaps reduce it a little.

Whilst training, your diet should be made up of as much as 65 per cent carbohydrate. Evidence suggests that training performance can be greatly affected if insufficient carbohydrates are consumed. Studies on athletes, such as the one above, have discovered what effect on glycogen stores a 30 per cent drop in carbohydrate can have. Over time, this carbohydrate deficiency could mean the difference between crossing the finishing line with a smile on your face and not finishing the race at all.

Glycaemic Index
The theory behind the glycaemic index was first put forward and developed by Dr David Jenkins, in an effort to help diabetics stabi-

lize their blood sugar levels. Not only are the principles behind the glycaemic index essential to diabetics, but runners can also benefit from having a better understanding; it will help them to choose the correct types of carbohydrates at certain times of the day.

Put simply, the glycaemic index measures the magnitude of the blood sugar response to different foods. Whenever we eat, our body has an insulin response to each type of food and in this case the varying types of carbohydrate. For example, when we eat meat our insulin response is minimal as meat contains negligible amounts of carbohydrate. However, glucose, the simplest form of carbo-

---

The Glycaemic Index

The glycaemic index (GI) response of carbohydrate-rich foods is heavily influenced by the other types of food eaten in conjunction with them. For example, if you eat a bowl of white pasta (which has a GI of 72) with a creamy and meaty sauce the insulin response will not be as great as it would be if you had eaten the pasta on its own, as other hormones have a direct effect on the amount of insulin secreted.

High Glycaemic Foods (60–100%)					
Bread		*Cereals*		*Fruit*	
Dark rye	76	Corn-flakes	83	Water-melon	72
White wheat	72	Shredded wheat	69	Pineapple	65
Whole wheat	69	Rice crispies	82	Banana	60
Cornmeal	68	Swiss muesli	60	Raisins	60
Baked Goods		*Grain*		*Vegetables*	
Rice Cakes	92	White rice	92	Baked potato	83
Doughnut	76	Cous cous	65	Mashed potato	75
Croissant	67	Corn-meal	68	Carrots	74
Sugars					
Glucose	100				
Honey	68				

A runner with suspected hypoglycaemia.

hydrate, produces a large insulin response. It is the body's response to glucose on which the glycaemic index is based and which all foods are compared to. On the glycaemic index, glucose has a rating of 100 and is the food that makes the body secrete the largest amount of insulin.

The GI and the Endurance Runner

Applying the principles of the glycaemic index to the runner is slightly different to that of the more sedentary person. Whereas foods high on the glycaemic index should be avoided by less active people to avoid weight gain and maintain a constant blood sugar level, for people who exercise regularly consuming high GI foods after a training run is actually beneficial to help maximize glycogen storage. This is due to the body's need to quickly replenish carbohydrate stores immediately after exercise. Foods high in GI are absorbed that much more quickly into the bloodstream, helping to restock the glycogen lost during the run.

Eating a snack high in GI, such as a banana or a glucose-rich energy drink, immediately after a hard or long run is a fantastic way to reintroduce lost carbohydrate.

Ideal food choices immediately after a run:

A few pieces of fruit, preferably high GI.
A slice of bread/toast with jam or honey.
An energy bar high in carbohydrate.

Low Glycaemic Foods (below 60%)					
Bread		*Cereals*		*Fruits*	
Pitta	57	Special K	54	Mango	55
Wholewheat pitta	55	All Bran	44	Grapes	46
Whole rye	52	Rice bran	20	Orange	43
Pumpernickel	49	Porridge oats	49	Apple	36
				Grapefruit	23
				Pear	36
				Strawberry	32
				Peach	42
				Plum	24
Baked goods		*Grains*			
Danish pastry	59	Brown rice	57		
Bran muffin	59	Whole rye	34		
Banana cake	50	Noodles	48		
Vegetables		*Legumes*		*Beverages*	
Tomato	38	Baked beans	48	Orange juice	57
Cucumber	24	Green beans	30	Pineapple	46
Green Peas	48	Kidney beans	27	Milk	28
Broccoli	very low			Tea	0
Cauliflower	very low			Coffee	0
Cabbage	very low				
Lettuce	very low				
Peppers	very low				
Onions	very low				
Sugars					
Fructose	23				
Lactose	46				

(Reproduced with the kind permission of Michael Colgan, from his book Optimum Sports Nutrition.*)*

Hypoglycaemia

Carbohydrates clearly play a significant role in keeping the body sufficiently fuelled for training runs and the race itself. Neglecting them will severely affect your performance, and possibly even your health. Every year, runners pull up at marathons and half marathons at various points on the course suffering from hypoglycaemia, a condition brought on by a lack of sugar in the bloodstream. The symptoms include:

- dizziness;
- confusion;
- headaches;
- disorientation;
- heavy legs;
- severe lethargy and fatigue;
- fainting.

Symptoms like these are unpleasant whilst at rest, let alone when you are competing in an event you may never do again. All steps must be taken to avoid hypoglycaemia during the race. Your determination may drive you through the initial warning signs but when there is no sugar left in the blood and the body is trying in vain to break down fat and protein quickly enough to produce sugar to feed your brain, you can black out and potentially drop into a diabetic coma.

Along with ensuring that you have got your pre-race carbohydrate intake correct, measures can be taken whilst you are running to help stop blood sugar levels dropping too low. These include:

- Take advantage of the sports drink stations.
- Consume a carbohydrate gel with water every 45 minutes.
- Snack on easily edible sugary sweets, such as jelly beans or jelly babies.

Whichever method you choose to prevent hypoglycaemia, it is important that you prac-tise during your training. If you decide to try a gel for the first time on race day and it doesn't agree with you, the only running you could be doing is straight to a toilet.

If you are diabetic, it is strongly advised that you consult your physician prior to training.

Getting your carbohydrate intake right throughout your preparations is clearly important and something that should not be taken for granted. If you ever experience symptoms of hypoglycaemia on a long run you will fully appreciate how important carbohydrates are to the endurance runner. I learnt my lesson early on in my career when I fainted whilst on a run with a client. The embarrassment of her then running ahead to her car to pick me up was enough to remind me never to go out for another run without eating properly.

It is not only poor carbohydrate management that affects the performance of many amateur runners. Insufficient and incorrect fluid intake can also have a major impact on the performance and health of a runner. This impact is so significant that the next chapter is dedicated solely to the importance of fluids.

VITAMIN AND MINERAL SUPPLEMENTATION

Vitamins and minerals are generally regarded to be the 'nuts and bolts' of nutrition. They are an essential part of our make-up and without them we would be unable to survive, let alone run.

Many runners ask whether they should be taking vitamin and mineral supplements. Although professional athletes certainly benefit from taking a variety of nutritional supplements, the advice given to the average runner by the majority of exercise specialists is usually the same. Generally speaking, if an individual's diet is balanced and of high quality, with plenty of fresh fruit and vegetables, sufficient quantities of essential vitamins and minerals are being consumed to meet

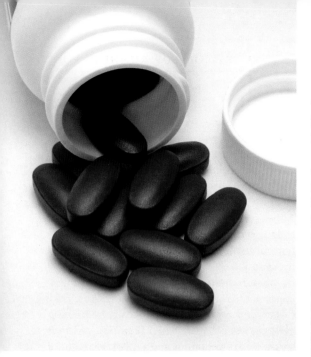

Vitamin and mineral supplements.

the body's demands. Despite high levels of activity, the vitamin and mineral status of an endurance runner is believed to be negligibly affected, questioning the need for supplementation. However, as an insurance policy there is certainly no harm in supplementing your diet with a multivitamin to ensure your vitamin and mineral status is maximized.

For the endurance runner, although all vitamins and minerals are important, some play a more important role than others. The remainder of this chapter looks at the most important vitamins and minerals and their role in the body.

Vitamins

It is rare for anyone in the western world to suffer any form of vitamin deficiency, but to ensure optimum running performance and health particular attention must be paid to the following.

The B Vitamins
The major B vitamins are B1 (thiamine), B2 (riboflavin), B3 (niacin), B5 (pyridoxine), B6 (pantothenic acid) and B12 (cobalmin).

There are others, including B15 and B17, but little is known about how they affect the body.

Generally regarded as the energy-providing vitamins, the Bs help to extract energy from fat, protein and carbohydrate. They can be found in a wide range of food, such as meat products, grains and vegetables; so as long as a balanced diet is followed, sufficient amounts of the B vitamins should be consumed.

> It is worth noting that when taken in high doses, such as in a supplement riboflavin (B2), B vitamins can make your urine turn a bright yellow colour. This must not be confused with dark yellow urine, which can indicate dehydration.

Vitamin C
Perhaps the best known of all the vitamins, vitamin C plays a vital role in a number of physiological processes. Vitamin C is necessary for:

- keeping the immune system healthy;
- the synthesis of collagen (the protein that makes tendons and ligaments);
- helping with the absorption of iron;
- its role as an antioxidant – essential for the athlete.

The suggested daily requirements of vitamin C are continuously under debate. Some argue that the amount consumed in our diets is sufficient, but others maintain that large doses are needed to help ward off infection, strengthen the immune system and even help to fight cancer.

If you had to choose one vitamin supplement to take as part of your endurance training, my advice would be to choose vitamin C. Doses of 1,000–2,000mg may seem excessive when the recommended daily allowance is just 60mg, but evidence suggests that this is the optimum level for a positive effect on your health.

Due to the regularity of an endurance runner's training, the body's immune system is depressed slightly after a run. It is for this reason that many top runners are vulnerable to colds and upper respiratory tract infections. By supplementing your diet with vitamin C, your immune system is strengthened, helping to ward off any viruses.

Minerals

Minerals play a variety of roles in the body, from transporting oxygen in the blood to ensuring the skeletal and muscular structures of the body are strong. Like vitamins, severe deficiency of minerals in the western world is rare but long distance runners are more vulnerable to deficiency than most. The following minerals have a particular significance to the runner, but before you consider mineral supplementation it is strongly advised that you do so in conjunction with professional advice. Excessive amounts of certain minerals in the body can be just as harmful as deficiency.

Iron

Iron is essential for the transportation of oxygen in the blood which, needless to say, is particularly important to the runner. Low levels of iron in the blood, known as anaemia, produce symptoms of fatigue, low energy levels and sleepiness, culminating in a drop in running performance.

Iron is consumed in the diet in two different forms, known as heme, found in meat products, and non-heme found in vegetable and fruit products. The major difference between the two is the differing absorption rates once they are eaten. As much as 40 per cent of the heme iron from meat is absorbed, whereas non-heme foods can have an absorption rate of as little as 5 per cent. It is because of this that vegetarians and those who consume small amounts of meat should be particularly aware of the risk of becoming anaemic.

As with all other minerals, supplementing your diet with extra iron should only be considered if you have first consulted with a nutritionist or your doctor. Trying to diagnose anaemia yourself and supplementing

Vitamin C helps to boost immunity.

Tomatoes are a rich source of vitamins and minerals.

with iron supplements can be dangerous as an excess of dietary iron makes you more vulnerable to infections.

To help increase your absorption of iron try to avoid caffeine products, which inhibit absorption further, and supplement your diet with vitamin C, which helps to increase absorption rates.

Calcium

Stored in the bones and the blood, calcium is important to keep bone structure strong and ensure the muscles contract effectively. So long as a balanced diet rich in dairy products and vegetables is followed it is highly unlikely that you will become calcium deficient, negating the need for any form of supplementation. As with iron, to ensure maximum

absorption try to avoid eating calcium-rich products with foods that inhibit absorption such as caffeine and cocoa.

Sodium

As discussed in the next chapter, a drop in blood sodium levels can bring on a sodium deficiency condition known as hyponatraemia leading to a potentially life-threatening coma. In everyday life, as with all the minerals, sodium levels are carefully regulated by the body's hormones. So long as the sodium in your diet is neither excessive nor limited, deficiency is highly unlikely.

To provide you with an overview of all the important vitamins and minerals, roles and deficiency symptoms, the table on pp111–113 can be used as a quick reference guide.

INFORMATION ON VITAMINS AND MINERALS

Vitamin	Solubility	RDA	Functions	Deficiencies and excesses	Sources
A	Fat soluble stored in body	Men: 5,000 units (RE retinal equivalents) Women: 4,000 units (800 RE) Toxic level: 10,000 to 50,000 units (2,000 to 10,000 RE) (if all from animal sources)	1. Formation of body tissue 2. Development of mucous secretions in nose, mouth digestive tract, organs (which show bacterial entry) 3. Development of visual purple in the retina of the eye, which allows one to see in the dark 4. Produces the enamel-producing cells of the teeth 5. Assists normal growth 6. Estrogen synthesis 7. Sperm production	Deficiencies can cause night blindness, damaged intestinal tract, damaged reproductive tract, scaly skin, poor bones, dry mucous membranes, and in children, poor enamel in the teeth. Toxic symptoms (of Retinol): may mimic brain tumour (increased pressure inside the skull), weight loss, irritability, loss of appetite, severe headaches, vomiting, itching, menstrual irregularities, diarrhoea, fatigue, skin lesions, bone and joint pains, loss of hair, liver and spleen enlargement, and insomnia. In children, overdose can stunt growth.	Butter and margarine, whole milk, liver, fish, fortified non-fat milk, fish-liver oils, egg yolk.
Beta-carotene	Water soluble	As antioxidant 25,000 to 50,000 units (15 to 30mg)	1. Precurser to vitamin A 2. Antioxidant – Reduces cancer risk – Reduces heart disease	Deficiency: Increased free oxygen radical activity. Excess: may yellow the skin	Carrots, broccoli, dark green or orange fruits or vegetables.
B1 (thiamin)	Water soluble	1.5mg (men) 1.2mg (women)	1. Metabolizes carbohydrates 2. Resulting glucose (sugar) nourishes muscles and nerves 3. Aids nerve functioning	Deficiencies can cause: mental depression, moodiness, quarrelsomeness and uncooperativeness, fatigue, irritability, lack of appetite, muscle cramps, constipation, nerve pains (due to degeneration of myelin sheath which covers the nerve), weakness and feeling of heaviness in the legs, beri-beri (a disease in which the muscles atrophy and become paralysed)	Liver, pork, yeast, organ meats, whole grains, bread, wheat germ, peanuts, milk, eggs, soya beans.

Vitamin	Solubility	RDA	Functions	Deficiencies and excesses	Sources
B2 (riboflavin)	Water soluble	1.8mg (men) 1.4mg (women)	1. Affects rate of growth and metabolic rate since it is necessary for the cell's use of protein, fat, and carbohydrate 2. Growth 3. Adrenal cortex activity 4. Red blood cells formation	Deficiencies can cause: burning and itching eyes, blurred and dim vision, eyes sensitive to light, inflammation of the lips and tongue, lesions at the edges of the mouth, digestive disturbances, greasy, scaly skin, personality problems	Eggs, liver and other organs, yeast, milk, whole grains, bread, wheat germ, green leafy vegetables
B3 (niacin or nicotinic acid)	Water soluble, stored in the body	20mg (men) 15mg (women)	1. Similar to riboflavin in metabolizing foods (especially sugars) 2. Maintain normal skin conditions 3. Aids in functioning of the gastro-intestinal tract	Deficiencies can cause: dermatitis (red, tender skin, becoming scaly and ulcerated), fatigue, sore mouth (tongue), diarrhoea, vomiting, nervous disturbances, mental depression, anorexia, weight loss, headache, backache, mental confusion, irritability, hallucinations, delusion of persecution, pellagra. Large doses can be toxic because it dilates blood vessels. Can cause skin flushing, dizziness, head throbbing, also dryness of skin, itching, brown skin pigmentation, decreased glucose (sugar) tolerance and perhaps a rise in uric acid in the blood	Yeast, liver, wheat, bran, peanuts, beans
Pantothenic acid	Water soluble. Little body storage	4–7mg	1. Carbohydrate, fat and protein metabolism 2. Synthesis of cholesterol and steroid hormones 3. Aids the functioning of the adrenal cortex 4. Aids in choline metabolism	Almost never deficient in human diets. Various animal studies have shown different results from deficiency: rough skin, diarrhoea, anaemia, possible coma, convulsions, hair loss, and many other symptoms. But they have not been shown in humans	Liver, organ meats, yeast, wheat bran, legumes, cereals

Vitamin	Solubility	RDA	Functions	Deficiencies and excesses	Sources
Biotin	Water soluble	0–3mg	Metabolism of amino acids, fatty acids and carbohydrates	Deficiencies are extremely rare. Raw egg whites, which combine with the biotin in the intestines and make it unavailable and some antibiotics (which kill the biotin-producing organization in the intestines) could cause a deficiency. Deficiency would be marked by: dry, scaly skin, grey pallor (skin colour), slight anaemia, muscular pains, weakness, depression and loss of appetite	Manufactured in the intestines. Also found in: liver, yeast, kidney, egg yolks
B6 (pyridoxine)	Water soluble	2.0mg (men) 2.0mg (women)	1. Catalyst in protein, fat, and carbohydrate metabolism. High protein diet increases the need for B6 2. Converts tryptophan to niacin 3. Assists in nervous system 4. Antibody production	Anaemia, dizziness, nausea, vomiting, irritability, confusion, kidney stones, skin and mucous membrane problems. In infants: irritability, muscle twitching, convulsions. Excesses – impaired sensation in limbs. Unsteady gait	Usually not necessary to supplement. Wheatgerm, kidney, liver, ham, organ meats, legumes, peanuts
Folic acid (folacin)	Water soluble	0.2–0.4mg	1. Aids in maturation of red and white blood cells 2. May assist in the synthesis of nucleic acids 3. DNA synthesis	Blood disorders, anaemia, diarrhoea. Deficiencies most likely to occur during pregnancy and lactation	Yeast, liver, egg yolk, green leafy vegetables
B12	Water soluble, stored in the body	60mg (men and women)	1. Controls blood forming defects and nerve involvement in pernicious anaemia 2. Involved in protein, fat, carbohydrates, nucleic acid and folic acid metabolism 3. Necessary to the normal functioning of cells, especially in the bone marrow, nervous system and intestinal tract	Sore tongue, amenorrhoea, signs of degeneration of the spinal cord, anaemia, heart, and stomach trouble, headache, and fatigue.	Liver, organ meats, oysters, salmon, eggs, beef, milk

Vitamin	Solubility	RDA	Functions	Deficiencies and excesses	Sources
C (ascorbic acid)	Water soluble. Little body storage	60mg; 10mg per day prevents scurvy Recommended as antioxidant: 1–1.5g	1. Forms collagen intracellular cement which strengthens cell walls (especially the small blood vessels and capillaries), tooth dentine, cartilage, bones and connective tissue 2. Aids in the absorption of iron 3. Aids in formation of red blood cells in the bone marrow 4. Aids in the metabolism of some amino acids (phenylalanine and tyrosine) 5. May be involved in the synthesis of steroid hormones from cholesterol 6. Any body stress may deplete the vitamin C in the tissues which may increase shock, or bacterial infections 7. Antioxidant	Scurvy results from low vitamin C intake. Minor symptoms of vitamin C deficiency could be: subcutaneous haemorrhages (bleeding below the skin), bleeding from gums, swollen gums. Excess of vitamin C can result in kidney stones and diarrhoea, destruction of B12, acidosis	Citrus, fresh fruits, berries, broccoli, tomatoes, green leafy vegetables, baked potatoes, turnips
D	Stored in liver Fat soluble	400 units (10mcgm) Toxic level: 1,000 to 1,500 units (25 to 38mcgm)	1. Assists in the development of bone and teeth by aiding calcium to harden 2. Facilitates the absorption of calcium and phosphorus, lack of which can cause muscular cramping. 3. Neuromuscular activity	Deficiencies: rickets (children), osteomalacia (women who have had frequent pregnancies and poor diets). Teeth may be more susceptible to caries (cavities). Cramping in muscles if there is a low level of calcium or phosphorus in the blood. Soft bones, bowed legs, poor posture. Toxic symptoms: fatigue, weight loss, nausea, vomiting, weakness, headache, kidney damage, kidney	Exposure to ultraviolet light (sunshine) can give minimum daily requirements by changing one type of cholesterol to vitamin D. Milk, fish-liver oils, egg yolk, butter, whole milk. Non-fat milk (with D) Margarines (with D added)

vitamin	Solubility	RDA	Functions	Deficiencies and excesses	Sources
D *continued*				stones, hardening of the soft tissue of the heart, blood vessels, lungs, stomach and kidneys. Increase cholesterol level of blood. Makes bones more fragile. High levels in developing foetuses and young children may cause mental retardation or blood vessel retardation or blood vessel malformation (especially a blockage in the aorta – the major artery from the heart)	
E (tocopherol)	Fat soluble Not stored in body	10 units 10mg TE (tocopherol equivalents) As an antioxidant: 400 units (TE) 600 units (if over 50 years, 2,500 if heavy exerciser)	1. It is thought to stabilize membranes 2. May be helpful in stabilizing Vitamin A 3. May be necessary in diets high in polyunsaturated fats 4. Aids in synthesizing red blood cells 5. Antioxidant	No known deficiency symptoms in human adults. Some premature infants apparently do not immediately develop the ability to absorb the vitamin	Synthesized in the intestines. Alpha tocopherol D Alpha tocopherol E better than mixed tocopherol E. Human milk (cow's milk poor), margarine, oil salad dressing, cereal germ, green leafy vegetables
K	Stored in liver Fat soluble	Men: 80mcgm. Women 63mcgm	Helps in the production of prothrombin (blood clotting agent)	Antibiotics taken orally (which could kill the synthesizing bacteria) or diarrhoea (which could flush out the bacteria) could possibly cause a deficiency. Newborn infants, especially premature babies, often suffer from a deficiency. This may cause excessive bleeding. Toxic symptoms in infants: jaundice, mild anaemia	Synthesized by intestinal bacteria. Green leafy vegetables, cabbage, cauliflower. Smaller amounts in: tomatoes, egg yolk and whole milk

Mineral	Solubility	RDA	Functions	Deficiencies and excesses	Sources
Calcium		1,200mg	Development of strong bones and teeth. Helps muscles contract and relax normally, utilization of iron. Normal blood clotting. Maintenance of body neutrality. Normal action of heart muscle	Rickets, porous bones, bowed legs, stunted growth, slow clotting of blood, poor tooth formation, tetany	Milk, cheese, mustard, turnip, green, clams, oyster, broccoli, cauliflower, cabbage, molasses, nuts. Small amount in egg, carrot, celery, orange, grapefruit, figs, and bread made with milk
Fluorine		1.5–4mg	Resistance to dental caries. Deposition of bone calcium. May be involved in iron absorption	Deficiencies: weak teeth and bones, anaemia, impaired growth. At levels of 1.5 to 4 parts per million teeth will be strong, but may be mottled. At levels over 6ppm teeth and bones may be deformed	Water supply containing 1ppm. Small amounts in many foods
Iodine		0.15mg	Constituent of thyroxin which is a regulator of metabolism Synthesis of vitamin A.	Enlarged thyroid gland. Low metabolic rate, stunted growth, retarded mental growth	Iodized salt sea foods, food gown in non-goitrous regions
Iron		10 mg (men) 15 mg (women)	Constituent of haemoglobin, which carries oxygen to the tissues. Collagen synthesis, antibody production	Nutritional anaemia, pallor, weight loss, fatigue, weakness, retarded growth	Red meats, especially liver, green vegetables, yellow fruits, prunes, raisin, legumes, whole grain and enriched cereals, molasses, egg yolk, potatoes, oysters
Magnesium		350–400mg (men) 280–300mg (women)	Activates various enzymes. Assists in breakdown of phosphate and glucose necessary for muscle contractions. Regulates body temperature. Assists in synthesizing protein. Tooth enamel stability	Failure to grow, pallor, weakness, irritability of nerves and muscles, irregular heartbeat, heart and kidney damage, convulsions and seizures, delirium, depressions	Soya flour, whole wheat, oatmeal, peas, brown rice, whole corn, beans, nuts, soybeans, spinach, clams

Mineral	Solubility	RDA	Functions	Deficiencies and excesses	Sources
Phosphorus		800–1,200mg (men & women)	Development of bones and teeth. Multiplication of cells. Activation of some enzymes and vitamins. Maintenance of body neutrality. Participates in carbohydrate metabolism. ADP/ATP synthesis acid/base balance. DNA/RNA synthesis	Rickets, porous bones, bowed legs, stunted growth, poor tooth formation. Excesses of phosphorus may have same effect on the bones as deficient calcium (osteoporosis porous bones)	Milk, cheese, meat, egg yolk, fish, nuts, whole grain cereals, legumes, soya flour, whole wheat, oatmeal, peas, brown rice, whole corn, beans
Potassium		2.5g	Acid-base balance. Carbohydrate metabolism. Conduction of nerve impulses. Contraction of muscle fibres. May assist in lowering blood pressure (if consumed in equal proportions as sodium)	Apathy, muscular weakness, poor gastro-intestinal tone, respiratory muscle failure, tachycardia (irregular heartbeat); cardiac arrest (heart stops beating)	Soya beans, cantaloupe, sweet potatoes, avocado, raisins, banana, halibut, sole, baked beans, molasses, ham, mushroom, beef, white potatoes, tomatoes, kale, radishes, prune juice, nuts and seeds, wheat germ, green leafy vegetables, cocoa, vegetable juices, cream of tartar, prunes, figs, apricots, oranges, grapefruit
Selenium		70mcgm men 55mcgm women As an antioxidant up to 100 for heavy exercisers	Antioxidant – may reduce risk of stomach and oesophageal cancers	Toxic level: nausea, hair loss, diarrhoea, irritability	Organ meats, meats, milk, fruits (depends on the amount of selenium in the soil)

Mineral	Solubility	RDA	Functions	Deficiencies and excesses	Sources
Sodium		1–2g (⅛ to ⅞ teaspoon)	Constraint of extra-cellular fluid. Maintenance of body neutrality. Osmotic pressure. Muscle and nerve irritability. Acid/base balance	Muscle cramps, weakness, headache, nausea, anorexia, vascular collapse. Excess may raise blood pressure	Sodium chloride (table salt), sodium bicarbonate (baking soda) monosodium glutamate. The greatest portion of sodium is provided by table salt and salt used in cooking. Foods high in sodium include: dried beef, ham, canned corned beef, bacon, wheat breads, salted crackers, flaked breakfast cereals, olives, cheese, butter, margarine, sausage, dried fish, canned vegetables, shellfish and salt water fish, raw celery, egg white
Zinc		15mg men 12mg women	Metabolism, formation of nucleic acid. Enzyme formation. Collagen production, fetal development, enhanced appetite and taste	Impaired growth, sexual development, skin problems	Beef, chicken, fish, beans, whole wheat, cashew nuts

RDA = Recommended (minimum) Daily Allowance

With the kind permission of D.L. Castill and J.M. Miller, International Journal of Sports Medicine 1980; 1: 2–14.

CHAPTER 11

Fluids: Balancing Fluids for Performance

Water contains no calories and few nutrients, so one could be forgiven for wondering why it is so essential for human performance. Second only to oxygen, water is the most important substance needed to sustain life. Without water our essential organs cannot function properly and blood cannot be pumped around the body. Just a 10 per cent decrease in our body weight through water loss can lead to death. To put this into perspective, we can afford to lose 40 per cent of our body weight in fat, protein and carbohydrate and still survive.

It is believed that the majority of sedentary people are dehydrated, simply because they do not take on the suggested daily amount of 1.5–2 litres of fluid per day. A rough indicator of whether you are hydrated is the colour of your urine. If you are adequately hydrated, your urine should be either clear or of a light straw colour; if you are dehydrated your urine has a stronger odour and is a deeper yellow colour. However, if you are taking a multivitamin tablet, a high dosage of vitamin B2 can turn your urine a bright yellow colour, which does not necessarily indicate dehydration.

So if you thought the most important part of endurance nutrition was loading up with carbohydrates – think again.

Water is essential for your preparations.

HYDRATION FACTS

- The human body consists of around 60–70 per cent water.
- Of our total daily intake of fluid, 60 per cent comes from water, 30 per cent from food and 10 per cent from the metabolic reactions within our body.
- During a marathon it is not uncommon to lose 6–8 per cent of body water content, despite taking on fluids during the race.
- A 2 per cent drop in hydration status leads to a significant rise in heart rate and core body temperature.
- A 5 per cent drop in hydration status can lead to a 30 per cent reduction in prolonged aerobic capacity.
- The muscles of a runner's legs during a marathon can produce as much as 17fl oz (500ml) of fluid in as little as 2–3 hours.

WHAT IS YOUR RATE OF FLUID LOSS?

The rate at which the human body loses fluid at rest and during a run varies from person to person. You may have noticed that during exercise your rate of perspiration may be more or less than a training partner who is running at the same intensity. As a result, it is essential that you find out early on in your training how much fluid you lose during a run so that you can take steps to reduce a significant drop in hydration status. The easiest way to give you an idea of your rate of fluid loss during a run is by simply using a set of bathroom scales.

Dehydration Test – The Bathroom Scales

Immediately before you embark on a run, step on your bathroom scales and jot down your exact weight. As soon as you return from your run, before you visit the bathroom or re-hydrate, step back on the scales and mark down your weight again. Your rate

Studies referenced by **William Costill and Jack Wilmore indicate that an 11 stone (70kg) runner will metabolize around 8oz (245g) of carbohydrate and lose as much as 2¹/₂ pints (1,500ml) during a one-hour run, with this figure rising in warm conditions. This fluid and carbohydrate loss can equate to a weight loss of as much as 4lb (2kg).**

of fluid loss during your run will vary enormously depending on the length of your run, ambient temperature and humidity. Although some of your weight loss will have come from lost glycogen and fat stores, the majority will be a result of fluid loss through respiration and perspiration.

By writing down your rate of fluid loss after runs of varying length, intensity and climate, you will be far better placed to know how much fluid you should be taking on during your race, whatever the conditions.

TIPS FOR MEASURING FLUID LOSS

- Always us the same scales in the same location to ensure accurate readings.
- Make a diary of your post-run weight loss.
- If you drink fluid during a run, take its weight into account when you weigh yourself afterwards.
- On race day, find out the expected conditions and refer back to your diary to see how much fluid you can expect to lose by comparing it to previous training runs in similar conditions.
- Once you have a rough idea of how much fluid you have lost, replace it as soon as possible. As a rough indicator, 1 pint (560ml) equals 1lb (450g).

A runner re-hydrates during a race.

The last few sips before the race.

DEHYDRATION AND RUNNING PERFORMANCE

Realizing that dehydration can have a detrimental effect on your running performance is clearly essential, but understanding the reason why performance is compromised is equally important. By developing an understanding of the effect dehydration has on your working tissues and organs, you will be better informed about the importance of replacing lost fluids.

Far too many runners are still competing in events without taking on sufficient fluids, not only endangering themselves but also ruining their participation in the event they have trained so hard to complete.

Fluid in the blood

Prior to exercise, the water content of the blood plasma is around 90 per cent. This high water content makes the blood free flowing, allowing the red blood cells to deliver essential nutrients to the working muscles. After prolonged exercise without replacing lost fluids, the water content of blood plasma is reduced, making the blood more viscous and harder to pump around the body. As a result, the heart rate must increase so that sufficient amounts of nutrient rich blood can reach the working muscles. If exercise continues without replacing lost fluids, the increased heart rate will take its toll on the body and running becomes impossible.

FLUID INTAKE GUIDELINES

As a rough guide, you should aim to drink the following quantities of fluid before and during a race:

- 14–20fl oz (400–600ml) two hours before a run;
- 5–10fl oz (150–300ml) in the last 20 minutes before a run (or 6ml per kg of body weight);
- 5–9fl oz (150–250ml) every 15–20 minutes during the run (on warm days you should aim for at least 9fl oz).

TIMING YOUR FLUID INTAKE

As well as those who ignore the importance of running whilst properly hydrated, there are also runners who can get a little carried away with taking on fluid. Timing and quantifying your fluid intake is something you need to practise whilst training, so that you can begin a race with the confidence that the fluid you drank in the lead-up to the starting gun is not going to want to be knocking on the walls of your bladder in the early stages of the race.

Throughout your training you should always think about making sure you are suffiiently hydrated several hours before your run. Use the 'pee' test mentioned previously to check out if you are sufficiently hydrated.

If you are embarking on a long early morning run, try these tips to maximize your hydration status:

- Try getting up a little earlier, to give yourself more time to hydrate.
- Set off with a runner-friendly water bottle so that you can re-hydrate on the run.
- Provided there isn't a frost, planting water bottles on your running route the evening before is the ideal solution to ensure you have regular water breaks. There will be regular water stations during your race, so why not practise drinking on the run during training?

Above all, come race day carry out the same procedures as in your training. Nerves will always be present in the hours leading up to a race, and the temptation to take anxious swigs of water is common. Once you have passed the 'pee test' and you are passing clear urine, you must stop drinking excessively. The odd mouthful to combat the nervous symptom of 'cotton mouth' (dry mouth) is fine, but your race plans could take a severe blow if you are looking for the toilet in the first few miles. To a degree, thanks to certain hormones, once you begin running the desire to urinate is depressed but excessive amounts of fluid will still make you need the bathroom.

The type of fluid you drink in the lead up to, during and after a run can have a significant impact on your hydration status and general performance. Water is perhaps the most obvious choice of drink but the popularity of sports drinks over the years has increased. Not only do they taste better than water, but scientific studies have clearly demonstrated that they can have a significant effect on our performance.

A typical sports drink supplied in events.

SPORTS DRINKS AND PERFORMANCE – FACT OR FICTION?

Decades ago, Lucozade completely turned the image of the sugary drink on its head. After being marketed as an essential drink for the elderly, it took a u-turn and marketed its product to athletes, highlighting how a glucose-rich beverage could enhance performance.

Many believed it was simply a marketing ploy, but research over the years has proven that sports drinks such as Lucozade and Gatorade play a vital role in maintaining not only hydration status but also blood sugar and electrolyte status. A variety of sports drinks is available to the runner, each with varying amounts of glucose.

After reading about the importance of carbohydrate in the previous chapter, the automatic assumption of many people is to choose the drink with the highest percentage of glucose to help maintain blood sugar levels. The truth is a little more complicated than that due to a function known as gastric emptying.

Gastric Emptying

Whenever we eat food or drink, the contents of the stomach and gastric juices are absorbed into the duodenum, where the nutrients are absorbed into the bloodstream and delivered to the working muscles. Gastric emptying is the movement of the contents of the stomach through to the duodenum. The time it takes for food to be broken down and absorbed is dependent on the type of food in the stomach.

In the case of sports drinks, the higher the glucose solution, the slower the rate of gastric emptying. A sports drink with a high sugar content consumed during exercise can take up to 2 hours to empty, compared to just 20 minutes for a weak sugar solution.

The Different Types of Sports Drink

Hypotonic
- 2–3g of sugar per 100ml;
- lower concentration than body fluids;
- absorbed quicker than water;
- fast rehydration.

Isotonic
- 5–7g of sugar per 100ml;
- similar concentration as body fluids;
- absorbed at the same speed as water.

Hypertonic
- 10g+ of sugar per 100ml;
- higher concentration than body fluids;
- slower absorption than water.

EFFECTIVE HYDRATION

For the quickest rate of fluid absorption and delivery of sugar to the bloodstream, the sports drink must be *isotonic* and contain a 5–7 per cent sugar content. Most sports drinks are manufactured with a variety of different sugars, such as glucose, fructose, corn syrup and maltodextrin, as this is believed to be more effective. To help aid sugar absorption, the sports drink must also contain electrolytes to maintain adequate levels of salt in the bloodstream.

Isotonic drinks are supplied at all endurance running events, so it is advisable to practise drinking them during your training to make sure your stomach can tolerate the

A carbo gel, to be taken every 45 minutes with water during a Marathon.

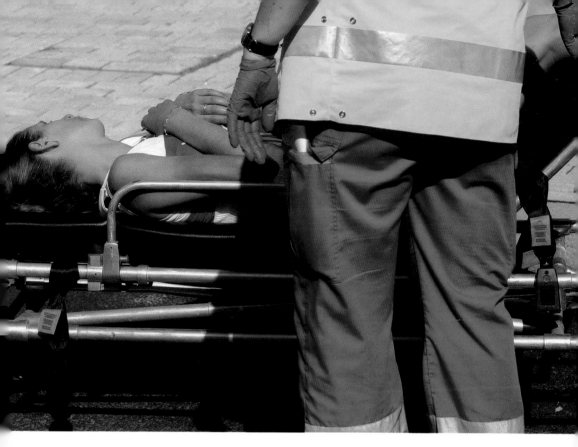

Hyponatremia can be seriously dangerous for your health.

formula. In most marathons, there are about five sports drinks stations and it is important that you visit every one of them. Not only will this help to keep you hydrated and your blood sugar levels elevated but the electrolytes are essential to avoid the potentially life threatening condition known as hyponatremia.

Electrolytes and Hyponatremia

One of the reasons why isotonic drinks are so effective is that they have a very similar composition to our body fluids, which contain glucose and electrolytes (salts). Electrolytes are the minerals sodium, chloride, potassium and magnesium and are all secreted in varying amounts in our sweat, especially sodium and chloride (hence our sweat tastes salty).

For exercise bouts lasting up to an hour, the effects of dehydration, electrolyte loss and low blood sugar should not significantly affect the health and performance of a runner

as long as a sensible nutrition plan has been followed. However, for endurance events in warm conditions where sweat losses are high, the risk of losing excessive amounts of electrolytes is increased significantly and symptoms of hyponatremia can occur.

During a marathon, fluid loss through sweat and respiration is high, initiating a sensation of thirst. Taking on water before and during the race may help to quench this thirst but the water can also detrimentally dilute the bodily fluids and lower their electrolyte content. With salt losses in the sweat, electrolyte loss can become so severe that hyponatremia can set in and make a runner very ill.

The symptoms of hyponatremia include:

- confusion;
- disorientation;
- nausea;
- weakness;
- seizures.

Caffeine is used by some people to boost performance.

Luckily, cases of hyponatremia are rare, but instances are reported every year where runners come close to death because they were unaware of the dangers that low sodium levels can have on the body.

Tips on How to Avoid Hyponatremia
- Avoid drinking excessive amounts of water on the morning of a race.
- Take advantage of the sports drink stations during the race.
- Do not deliberately avoid salty foods in the lead up to a race, but also ensure you do not consume excessive amounts.

CAFFEINE

The effect of caffeine consumption on our health has been highlighted in newspapers and magazines for years. It seems that when one 'scientific' report is released about the negative effects that caffeine has on our health the very next week another report is released contradicting the previous one and singing the praises of the health benefits of caffeine.

Caffeine is one of the world's most popular drugs, and when ingested it has a number of physiological effects on the body. As well as acting as a stimulant on the central nervous system, it also stimulates cardiac muscles and skeletal muscles through the body's handling of calcium. Even with doses as low as a single cup of coffee (30–100mg of caffeine) the effects on the body can be felt as soon as it enters the bloodstream.

Caffeine and Exercise

The ergogenic (performance enhancing) effect of caffeine has been well documented

> Remember that coffee is not the only drink that contains caffeine. Tea, stimulant drinks and cola all contain large amounts of caffeine.

in recent years and the evidence to support its positive influence on athletic performance is so compelling that the International Olympic Committee has made caffeine a restricted substance. Athletes with a high level of caffeine in their urine are assumed to have been doped and can be banned for years from competition.

Cases of athletes exceeding the allowed level of caffeine are rare, as the amount of coffee needed to be ingested to reach the banned limit is so excessive that the athlete's performance is likely to be impeded by gastrointestinal discomfort. However, the advent of caffeine tablets, which can provide up to 200mg of caffeine per pill, now makes ingestion of caffeine easier.

Despite high doses of caffeine being deemed illegal for competition, many runners swear by it as an essential supplement to increase performance. Although the placebo effect may play a role in this enhancement of performance, research does suggest that caffeine has a significant impact on the way we metabolize fats and carbohydrates during exercise.

The Physiological Effects of Caffeine During Exercise

Although research is ongoing, there is evidence to support the following facts about caffeine supplementation in the athlete:

- Varying doses of caffeine can have differing effects on the body, but ranges of 3–6mg per kg of bodyweight appear to be optimal.
- Caffeine is believed to increase fat oxidation, increasing the amount of fat available to be used as an energy source during exercise.

- Glycogen stores are thought to be spared by using caffeine, due to its ability to free up more of the body's fat stores.
- The optimum timing of caffeine intake is thought to be 60 minutes before exercise.

Negative Aspects of Caffeine Supplementation

It is clear that caffeine can provide significant benefits to a caffeine-responsive runner if the correct doses and timing of caffeine intake are followed. There are, however, a number of negative effects that caffeine can have on the body that could have a detrimental effect on performance. If you are considering using caffeine as an ergogenic aid, it is worth bearing in mind the following:

- Caffeine, like alcohol, has a diuretic effect on the body. If timed incorrectly, you find yourself needing the bathroom early on in a run.
- Irrespective of the benefits that caffeine can provide, if you drink coffee it must not be at the expense of water or a sports drink. This could mean you begin a run dehydrated.
- Excessive amounts of coffee can cause gastrointestinal discomfort, so care must be taken to ensure that your stomach is not uncomfortable at the beginning of a run.
- Coffee interferes with the absorption of iron, so if you are a regular coffee drinker make sure you consume iron-rich foods at a different time to your coffee intake.

Whether to use caffeine as an ergogenic aid is a decision you will have to make yourself, but it must not be taken lightly. Caffeine affects everyone slightly differently and some are more sensitive to its effects that others. Migraines, anxiety and nervousness are just some of the symptoms that excessive levels of caffeine can have on people.

If you want to experiment with caffeine supplementation, always try it out during your training to discover the effects it has on you. I would strongly advise you to take extreme caution if you choose to use high levels of caffeine – remember that it is a drug and it does not agree with some people. If in doubt, read more about the effects of caffeine consumption and if necessary consult your physician.

ALCOHOL

During your training, it is unrealistic to expect you to drink only water and sports drinks. You must have a social life too, to not only keep you sane but also so that you can drop into the conversation that you are in training for the marathon. During evenings out with friends, do not feel guilty about replacing your isotonic sports drink with a glass of full bodied Shiraz. Alcohol is not completely out of bounds, provided it is consumed in small amounts every now and again.

The ideal time to enjoy a glass of your favourite tipple is in the evening after your long training run. Ensure you have hydrated yourself well after the run and you'll find your favourite drink will taste all the better knowing that you thoroughly deserve it.

As alcohol is a diuretic it will make you need to go to the bathroom more regularly than if you were drinking water. This is because the alcohol inhibits the actions of a hormone in the body that regulates water balance.

Alcohol's diuretic effect is the reason why it is unwise to train the morning after you have had a few drinks. Even if you feel fine, your cells may not be well hydrated and your running performance may well be impaired. It can also be dangerous to exercise if you are already dehydrated. Alcohol is also responsible for depleting a number of vitamins such as B1, folic acid, B12 and vitamin C.

In the lead up to a race, most runners try to avoid all forms of alcohol to ensure they are as nutritionally prepared as possible. Although the occasional drink will do no significant harm, abstinence from alcohol in the weeks leading up to race day is strongly advised.

CHAPTER 12

Running Injuries: Their Diagnosis and Treatment

One inevitable consequence of pushing your body harder than it has ever been pushed before is that at one stage or another you are likely pick up an injury. Some niggles are nothing more than a minor inconvenience, making running uncomfortable but possible. Other injuries, if left untreated, can become chronic and if managed poorly can ruin your chances of making the start line, let alone the finish.

The probability of incurring an injury is just one of those things that you have to accept if you are preparing for an endurance running event, and common sense is needed when it comes to treating minor niggles to ensure they don't become big ones.

Injury prevention is clearly better than treatment once you are injured, so it is essential to follow the advice in this book with regard to correct running shoes, running frequency and taking time to rest. However, regardless of all the precautionary measures you can take, afflictions such as muscle tears, tendon inflammation and joint pain are all part and parcel of the joys of being a long distance runner. Be comforted by the knowledge that as you line up at the start of the biggest race of your life, with a few niggles here and there, you will most certainly not be alone.

njuries must be avoided at all costs.

ANATOMY OF THE RUNNER

To develop an understanding of the most common injuries, it helps if you know the names and locations of the major leg muscles. It is not essential that you remember the following information, but will be of interest to those wishing to learn more about the

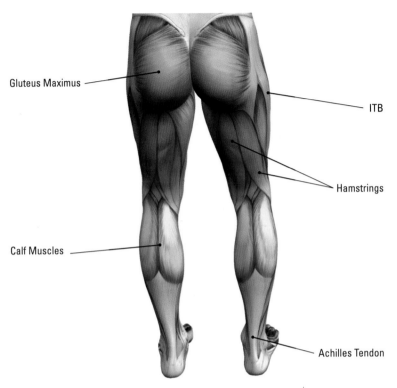

The muscles on the back of the legs.

Gluteus Maximus

ITB

Hamstrings

Calf Muscles

Achilles Tendon

anatomy of the lower body. In addition, over the course of your training you are bound to read or hear about typical injuries and muscles, so use this section to provide you with the basic understanding of what people are talking about when they claim to have a 'partial rupture' of their 'adductor brevis'.

The Leg Muscles: A Closer Look

The majority of people, even those who have little interest in exercise, have a degree of knowledge about certain leg muscles. Most people will have heard of muscles such as quadriceps (quads) and hamstrings, but few are aware that the bigger picture is a little more complex.

For example, informing a physiotherapist of the nature and cause of the discomfort in your hamstring muscle is useful information but he/she will first need to discover

which one of the three hamstring muscles damaged so that the appropriate course rehabilitation and treatment can be recon mended.

The list below outlines some of th commonly known leg muscle groups, an details the muscles and structures that mak up that group:

- quadriceps
  vastus medialis
  vastus intermedialis
  vastus lateralis
  rectus femoris
- hamstrings
  bicep femoris
  semi-membranosus
  semi-tendonosis
- calf muscles
  gastrocnemius
  soleus

The muscles on the front of the legs.

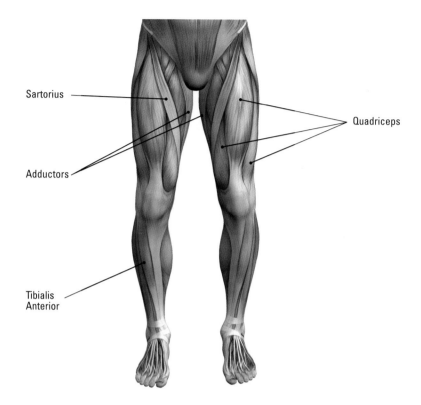

Sartorius

Quadriceps

Adductors

Tibialis Anterior

- adductors
  - *magnus*
  - *brevis*
  - *longus*
  - *gracilis*
- gluteals
  - *maximus*
  - *minimus*
  - *medius*

Other individual muscles, tendons and structures that are prone to injury include:

- Achilles tendon;
- tensor fascia lata (TFL);
- illio tibial band (ITB);
- tibialis posterior;
- tibialis anterior;
- peroneals;
- piriformis.

FINDING A THERAPIST

If an injury becomes a chronic problem and simply refuses to go away you should consult a professional. However, the dilemma faced by many runners is who to go to for treatment.

Physiotherapists, chiropractors, sports therapists, podiatrists and massage therapists are just a few of the specialists who commonly help to treat running injuries. Personal recommendation is without doubt the best form of referral. If a friend has been success-fully treated for an injury by a certain thera-pist, it is likely that they will also be able to help you.

Whoever you see to treat your injury, always make sure that they have the correct qualifications and insist on establishing what they believe the exact nature of your injury is and how long it is likely to take to heal. If your injury is similar to any of the conditions

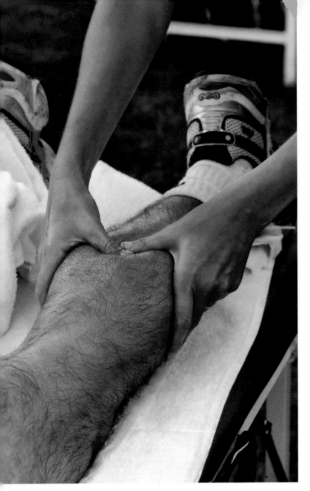

A runner having a sports massage.

mentioned below it is always a good idea to inform the therapist what you think it may be so that they realize you have a degree of knowledge about the subject.

Paying for treatment that is not working is not only frustrating but also means more time off training. If you feel your injury is not improving as quickly as you would expect, let your feelings be known to the therapist and if necessary seek a second opinion.

MUSCLE AND LIGAMENT INJURIES

Injuries resulting from your marathon preparations happen in a number of ways. Biomechanical problems in the lower leg from running on uneven surfaces or wearing incorrect shoes for your gait can sometimes take weeks to show themselves. An accumulation of stress on imbalanced muscles may initially show no painful symptoms, but over time leg or foot discomfort becomes apparent and treatment is needed. When injuries are acute, such as a sudden muscle or ligament tear, pain can be felt instantly in the affected area. Depending on the severity of

The most popular injury practitioners, what they specialize in and how they approach injury rehabilitation		
Practitioner	*Specialism*	*Rehabilitation method*
Physiotherapist	Soft tissue injuries such as ligament, muscle and tendon tears.	Ultrasound, massage, stretching, some manipulation.
Chiropractor	Spinal manipulation, with an emphasis on correct spinal and pelvic alignment to help correct some biomechanical injuries.	Manipulation of the spine to correct vertebral and pelvic misalignments.
Podiatrist	Assessment of the lower body and feet to check correct gait and biomechanical function.	Stretching exercises for tight muscles and prescription of orthotics where necessary to correct over-pronation.
Massage therapist	Deep tissue massage to help elongate muscle fibres and disperse knotted muscles.	Hard massage using hands, knuckles and elbows to target and relax deep muscles. Special stretching techniques are also used.

the rupture, running can become impossible and a hobble is the most pain-free movement you can perform to get back home. Tearing muscles is not uncommon in running, but the severity of the tear dictates the prognosis of the injury.

The degree of muscle damage is generally classed as a 'grade' of tear:

Grade 1   A small number of muscle fibres are torn, causing minor discomfort. There is little bleeding within the muscle, and normal function is possible.

Grade 2   A large number of fibres are torn, causing significant pain and an inability to walk properly. There is significant bleeding within the muscle, and palpation is painful. Muscle function is impaired.

Grade 3   A severe tear where the majority of the muscle fibres are ruptured. There is a large degree of bleeding, which can spread over a large area. Muscle movement is impaired and the pain is excruciating, especially to touch.

Grade 4   A complete muscle rupture is highly unlikely in an endurance runner. The muscle is completely torn away from the bone and a 'snapping' sound can sometimes be heard. If you do completely rupture a muscle, you will certainly know about it.

Treatment of a Muscle Tear

Whichever grade of muscle tear you incur (and let's hope it's not a grade 4), the treatment in the acute stage (the first 48–72 hours) is the same. The well-known acronym 'RICE' must come into play immediately to begin the rehabilitation process:

R est   Avoid training for 48–72hours to allow any muscle bleeding to stop, and prevent further muscle damage.

I ce   Apply an ice pack or a bag of frozen peas to the injured muscle. This helps to narrow the capillaries and stop the muscle from bleeding.

C ompression   Use a bandage or a piece of tight clothing to compress the muscle. This helps to reduce swelling and bleeding.

E levation   By elevating the injured muscle above your heart blood flow to the bleeding muscle is reduced, aiding the healing process.

If after two to three days the muscle is still uncomfortable to walk on and the prospect of resuming your training programme any time soon looks doubtful, it is strongly advised that you seek professional help. A single trip to a specialist will enable you to establish the best form of treatment and rehabilitation to get you back on the road as soon as possible. A series of stretching and strengthening exercises, combined with heat treatment in the chronic stages of the injury, invariably help to accelerate the healing process but expert advice is essential to ensure that the correct treatment is prescribed.

Treatment of a Ligament Tear

A ligament tear is fairly rare among runners, as the running movement itself does not place nearly as much stress on the ligaments as it does on muscle tissue. Ligaments are white, fibrous structures that connect bone to bone, ensuring that the skeletal system is 'bound' together properly. The ankle is the most likely location of a ligament injury whilst running, and the most likely cause is running on uneven ground.

The severity of a ligament tear is assessed using the same grading system as for muscles, and treatment guidelines of a ligament injury are also identical to that of a muscle rupture. The one significant difference between the

The sites of ITB pain.

healing process of muscles and ligaments is the limited availability of blood to the ligaments. Ligaments are known as avascular structures, and blood flow to them is minimal. Blood is essential to recovery, as it provides the nutrients required for repair. Therefore, ligaments can take significantly longer to recover than the more vascular muscles. Heat treatment in the chronic stages of rehabilitation helps to attract more blood to the area to speed recovery, but once again professional advice is strongly recommended.

COMMON INJURIES TO LOOK OUT FOR

It is almost a given that the majority of runners will experience a minor muscle tear at some stage of their training, but because the degree of damage is small you can still go running. However, certain injuries have a tendency of cropping up more often than others and, if left untreated, they can develop into long-term problems.

Over the years I have had little option but to be strict with clients who insist on running whilst carrying certain injuries. The frustration at not being able to train for a week or two is understandable, but it is important to realize that those two weeks of rest invariably mean the difference between competing in a race and being in too much pain to even consider starting.

The following injuries can severely hamper your marathon preparations if you choose to ignore the symptoms and carry on training:

- illio-tibial band syndrome;
- Achilles tendonitis;
- plantar fascitis;
- shin splints;
- piriformis syndrome.

Illio-tibial Band Syndrome

Also referred to as illio–tibial band friction syndrome, this injury occurs in just over 10 per cent of runners and can be incredibly frustrating and difficult to treat. If there is one injury where prevention is better than a cure then this is the one.

The illio-tibial band is a non-elastic cord stretching from the TFL, just below the pelvis, to below the outside (lateral) of the knee. If this band becomes excessively tight it can cause friction on the outside of the knee and even in the hip joint, causing a great deal of discomfort. Pain is usually experienced on the outside of the knee when it is flexed, and it is sore to touch. In mild cases, after initial discomfort you may feel ready to go for a jog, only for symptoms to reappear after a few miles as the ITB begins to tighten.

Symptoms
- Discomfort on the outside of the knee or hip;
- a 'clicking' sensation on knee flexion on the outside of the knee as the tendon rubs against the bone;
- pain in the knee or hip when attempting to walk downstairs and sometimes when sitting down in a low chair;
- sudden onset of pain several miles into a run.

Causes
There are a number of causes of ITB syndrome and it can affect any runner, regardless of sex, age or fitness levels. The main causes include:

- running on a cambered or uneven surface;
- upping your running mileage too quickly;
- increasing the intensity of your runs;
- incorrect running shoes for your gait;
- muscular imbalance in the legs.

All of these factors result in the ITB tightening and rubbing against skeletal structures, causing inflammation and considerable discomfort.

Prevention
The most effective way to avoid contracting ITB syndrome is to make sure you follow all of the training advice mentioned earlier in the book. Simple measures like a gradual increase in weekly mileage, choosing the right shoes for your gait and following a stretching regime will help to reduce your chances of picking up this very painful and stubborn injury.

Treatment
If you are unfortunate enough to experience the symptoms of ITB syndrome, the first thing you must do is follow the RICE protocol, especially the application of ice to help reduce inflammation. Professional advice is really the only option, in order to confirm the diagnosis. Rehabilitation exercises, such as stretching of specific muscles, can be effectively administered.

Whilst you are living with the injury and running is not possible, you may find that other forms of aerobic exercise such as swimming, cycling and rowing can be undertaken. If this is the case, substitute your running for one of these to keep your fitness levels up.

Achilles Tendonitis

The Achilles tendon is a very thick tendon that connects the calf muscle to the heel. Throughout your training it is worked incredibly hard and injuries to it are not uncommon. Achilles tendonitis, literally meaning 'inflammation of the Achilles tendon', involves the degeneration of the tendon and is particularly common in men.

Many runners make the unforgivable mistake of ignoring initial symptoms and soldiering on with their training programme, hoping that the pain will pass. The use of anti-inflammatory medication may well help to mask the discomfort, but by continuing to run with an Achilles injury, you might as well end any ideas you have of competing in an event.

Symptoms
- Stiffness in the Achilles tendon, especially in the morning;
- pain when trying to stand on tip-toe;
- gradual onset of discomfort during and after exercise;
- significant tenderness to touch.

Causes
The main causes of Achilles tendonitis are very similar to that of ITB syndrome. A sudden increase in running distance or intensity can place the Achilles tendon under a level of stress that it is simply not used to, initiating an inflammatory response. Incorrect footwear with poor shock absorption, and excessive pronation, can also be contributory factors, so once again you should try to prevent the condition rather than having it treated once contracted.

Common locations of Achilles tendon pain.

Prevention

This injury, once contracted, can stay with you for a long period of time, so prevention is your priority. The key steps you can take to protect your Achilles tendon from injury are:

Make sure you have the correct trainers for your running gait.
Warm up well before a run with a brisk walk.
• Stretch out the calf muscles well before and after a run.
• Do not increase your running intensity and/or speed too quickly.
Avoid over-training.

Treatment

If you begin to feel a niggle in your Achilles tendon, the first thing you must do is apply ice to the area and keep icing it for 48–72 hours. Even if you feel it is over the top, keep icing. You must reduce the inflammation as soon as possible.

Regular stretches for the calf muscle are an important part of rehabilitation, but they must be performed gently to avoid further aggravation. Taking professional advice, irrespective of injury severity, is recommended so that your specific injury can be assessed and treatment can be administered accordingly.

Plantar Fasciitis

The foot contains a vast number of complex structures. Small bones, ligaments and tendons all work harmoniously together to create a smooth and pain-free running stride. The repetitive nature of endurance running can, however, initiate a variety of inflammatory responses, of which plantar fasciitis is one.

Running underneath the foot, from the bottom of the heel bone to the toes, is a long, fibrous tissue known as the fascia. This elastic sheath can sometimes become inflamed and cause a great deal of discomfort.

Symptoms

• Pain in the bottom of the heel, especially in the morning;
• pain feels like 'stepping on a stone';
• a burning sensation in the arch of the foot;
• relief can be felt when standing on the heels.

Causes

Predictably, as with most other injuries, plantar fasciitis can be caused by over-pronation, tight calf muscles, over-training and increasing your training intensity too quickly.

Prevention

A good warm-up and stretch prior to a run will ensure that the muscles are properly prepared for a run and that tightness does not have a knock-on effect on the plantar fascia. Taking time to stretch after a run is also important as it ensures that the muscle fibres are stretched out and realigned. Resisting the temptation to train harder than your body and muscles are ready for is also a good precautionary measure.

Treatment

As with any inflammatory injury, the RICE protocol must be followed at the onset of any plantar fascia discomfort. Under no circumstances should running be resumed until symptoms have disappeared. In cases of chronic (long-term) pain, the advice of a professional should be considered so that a biomechanical assessment can be carried out. If the root cause of the injury is excessive over-pronation, shoe inserts can be prescribed to reduce the stress and over-stretching of the plantar fascia.

Shin Splints

The term 'shin splints' is used to describe any discomfort in the lower leg. There are, however, several varieties of shin splint, and their diagnosis and treatment is dependent on the location of pain. Shin splints are generally categorized as either anterior compartment syndrome or posterior compartment syndrome.

Anterior Compartment Syndrome

If discomfort is felt during or after a run at the front (anterior) of the lower leg, it is likely that you have anterior compartment syndrome. The muscles at the front of the shin can become tender to touch, and especially sore when the feet are lifted upwards against resistance.

Symptoms
- Soreness on the muscle situated immediately next to the shin bone;
- pain in the anterior muscles when running and when the feet are lifted upwards;
- weakness in the anterior muscles, felt when trying to lift the feet up.

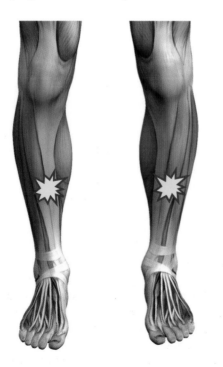

The common locations of shin splint pain.

Causes
A sudden increase in running intensity and change in running surface are major contributors to anterior compartment syndrome. Switching from running on grass to running on roads causes the muscles in the lower leg to be used slightly differently, leading to a fast rate of muscle swelling within the sheath of the lower leg. This swelling increases pressure within the anterior compartment of the lower leg and can cause significant discomfort.

Prevention
Along with ensuring that the correct footwear is being used and running frequency and intensity do not rise too sharply, thought must be given to a sudden change in running surface. Many new runners are concerned that excessive road running will inevitably lead to injury due to the shock that the hard surface inflicts on the joints. However, by performing the majority of training on soft surfaces such as grass and then suddenly introducing a distance run on the road, the chances of contracting anterior compartment syndrome are high. Alternating the surface that you run on is by no means off-limits, but a gradual transition is advised to allow the anterior shin muscles to adapt to the change in surface.

Treatment
RICE (page 133) is the first course of action to reduce any muscle swelling and inflammation. Avoid running for a number of days or until pain has gone. If symptoms recur, seek professional advice and have your gait assessed. You may need orthotics in your shoes to correct an over-pronating running gait.

Posterior Compartment Syndrome and Medial Tibial Stress Syndrome

Due to the number of muscles situated in the posterior (rear) compartment of the lower leg, diagnosing the exact cause of this particular form of shin splint can be difficult. Although pain experienced in the calf region of the lower leg can be classed as a form of posterior compartment syndrome, by far the most common form experienced by runners, and the type to look at in more detail, is medial tibial stress syndrome.

Symptoms
- Depending on the exact cause and structure affected, pain can be felt on the shin bone (tibia) or the muscles on the medial (inside) of it;
- pain on the tibia bone may indicate a stress fracture;.
- pain on running, which may dissipate after a while.
- in the advanced stage, discomfort can be felt whilst walking and at rest;
- pain can be initiated by standing on tip toe.

Causes
Over-training, too many high-intensity runs and over-pronation can all cause any form of posterior compartment syndrome. Excessive running and sharp increases in weekly mileage can cause the muscles of the lower leg to pull on the fascia, which connects the muscles to the bone. Over time this can cause inflammation and chronic pain if running is continued. As with anterior compartment syndrome, a sudden swelling of the muscles within the posterior sheath can cause a build-up of pressure and can contribute to lower leg pain.

Prevention
All normal injury prevention guidelines must be followed to avoid being inflicted with this debilitating condition. A sensible approach to training, wearing proper footwear and avoiding any sudden change in training patterns are essential to avoid your running programme being disrupted by lower leg pain.

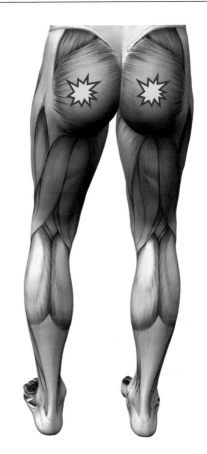

Piriformis pain is felt deep in the buttock.

Treatment
After the area has been treated with the RICE procedure, avoid running or any activity that induces pain. If symptoms continue, seek treatment by a professional. They may recommend the use of shoe orthotics.

Piriformis Syndrome

The piriformis is a very deep muscle in the buttocks, running from the lower spine (sacrum) to the top of the thigh bone near the hip joint. The piriformis acts as a stabilizing muscle during running, but due to its sensitivity in some people it can go into spasm, causing discomfort deep in the buttocks, and the pain can even radiate into the lower back.

To add another complication, the large sciatic nerve that runs from the lower back all the way down the leg passes through the 'sciatic notch' in the pelvis, sharing a small space with the piriformis muscle. If the piriformis is aggravated and becomes inflamed it can interfere with the sciatic nerve and cause a great deal of pain in the buttocks and the leg.

Symptoms
- Intense pain felt in the central deep part of the buttock;
- occasionally, referred pain and stiffness can be experienced in the lower back;
- when the sciatic nerve is involved, pain can also be felt in the back of the leg.

Causes
The specific reasons why some people experience pain in the piriformis are not fully understood; however, women appear to be more prone than men. People with a history of lower back pain may be more susceptible, but the reality is that anyone can experience discomfort of the piriformis, even non runners.

Prevention
Regular and thorough stretching exercise specifically for the piriformis can help to keep the muscle stretched and prevent it shortening, which will reduce the chances of it impinging on the sciatic nerve. A good stretching routine before and after exercise as well as during the day is strongly advised. For advice on how to stretch your piriformis, see page 57.

Treatment
Stretching the piriformis is the best thing you can do to help relieve the symptoms. Anti-inflammatory drugs can help but caution must be taken before you begin popping pills. Perhaps the most effective form of treatment is a sports or deep tissue massage.

Through special techniques, a properly qualified massage therapist will be able to perform 'trigger pointing' procedures to help relax the muscle and provide significant pain relief. One word of caution, however; although trigger pointing techniques can give you long-term relief, the procedure itself cannot be described as relaxing. Having a therapist pressing their elbow deep into the middle of your buttock is not what you would describe as pleasant, but the relief once it is over certainly makes it all worth while.

ACUTE AND SUPERFICIAL INJURIES

If you are lucky enough to escape the major biomechanical injuries such as the ones discussed above, it is likely that at some stage you will experience a less severe short-term affliction of some sort. Did you really think that running 13.1 or 26.2 miles was going to be 100 per cent trouble free?

One or more of the ailments that follow are experienced by nearly all runners at some stage of their training. Some are avoidable and some just go with the territory of being a long distance runner. Think of these injuries as war wounds and enjoy showing them off to your nearest and dearest. They may not appreciate it very much but it will certainly make your friends realize that endurance running is not for the faint hearted.

Blisters

If you are only going to experience one affliction, then it is likely to be the occasional blister. Caused by the friction of the skin against the socks or trainers, fluid can accumulate at the point of rubbing, making the skin sensitive and sore. Popping blisters is not generally advised, unless the pain is too intense, in which case a sterile needle can be used to pierce the skin and drain out the fluid.

As with all injuries, all attempts must be made to avoid contracting a blister in the first place. However, should you feel a blister coming on make sure the area is kept clean by using an antiseptic wipe and use a good quality plaster made specifically for blisters, to prevent further friction. Blisters are incredibly annoying, especially for those people who are prone to them, so try the following tips to help you run blister free:

- Apply petroleum jelly to the feet prior to a run. This helps to lubricate prone areas and reduce friction.
Buy good quality running socks. Poor quality cotton socks are a bad choice for runners, so spend that little bit more on specialist running socks to help reduce rubbing on the skin.
- Wear in new trainers slowly. New shoes take time to mould to your feet and can cause rubbing when new. *Never* use a new pair of trainers for race day of any long distance run; by the half-way mark you will certainly be hobbling.

Runner's Nipple

Although the most common friction injury is the blister, runner's nipple certainly wins the prize for the most eye-watering sight for spectators in the later stages of a race. You may not experience any discomfort during a short run, but after several hours of running if the nipples are not protected and the material of the running vest is coarse, they can begin to bleed and become incredibly sore.

Runner's nipple is more common in men due to the absence of a bra; therefore men should take some simple precautionary measures to prevent nipple rub, for the spectators' sake as well as their own. Simply sticking a plaster over each nipple is sufficient to prevent chafing, but you should first try this during training.

Black and Disappearing Toenails

The gradual darkening of toenails as your weekly mileage edges higher occurs because of the combination of your toes pounding the pavements and pushing at the front of your trainers. Over time, bruising and even blood blisters can develop under the toe nails, causing them to darken and in some cases eventually fall off. Some runners are more prone to this than others, so you may just have to accept that in the later stages of your training your toe nails are not going to be looking pretty in flip-flops. Other than making sure your trainers are not too small for your feet there is very little that you can do about black toenails, I'm afraid; you will just have to get used to it.

Cramp

When a muscle cramps, it enters a spasm and contracts violently. This intense muscular contraction can often make running impossible and the pain can be quite severe. From novice runners to the most experienced, cramp is a condition that can affect anyone, regardless of running ability or fitness levels. Over the years, the theories on the causes and treatment of cramp have varied but the exact causes are still largely unknown.

The most popular theories on the causes of cramp include:

- dehydration;
- imbalance of electrolytes;
- tight and un-stretched muscles;
- tired and fatigued muscles.

It is likely that cramp is in fact caused by one or a combination of the above theories, so in order to prevent cramp the best course of action is to follow the guidelines on proper hydration, electrolytes and stretching. This will significantly reduce your chances of being crippled by cramp mid-race.

Stitch

Theories about stitches have also been scruti-nized over the years and, like cramp, no one has provided a definitive answer as to why one minute we can be jogging along quite happily and then all of a sudden we are hit with a searing pain in our side.

Runners have consistently been advised to avoid eating a large meal prior to a run, to avoid a stitch. The theory behind this is twofold. The first is that a large quantity of food in the stomach whilst running causes a ligament to be overstretched, inducing the stitch pain. The second theory is that the blood supply demanded by the muscles during a run takes away the blood required by the digestive system to digest food. This competition and deprival of blood for food digestion can contribute to the stitch pain. More recently, it is thought that the pain from a stitch originates from the diaphragm as a result of fatigue. However, this does not explain the reason why runners can recover from a stitch after a period of perseverance.

Cramping often occurs in the latter stages of a run.

Along with avoiding a large meal prior to a run, making sure that you have used the toilet (fully) before setting off is believed to help fend off the dreaded stitch. If, however you do feel the symptoms of a dull ache on the right-hand side of your rib cage during a run, try the following tips:

- lean forwards slightly and breathe through pursed lips;
- breathe deeply and slowly;
- place your hands on your head or hips for a few hundred metres.

Runner's Trots

Changing the label for this condition does not make the experience any more comfortable. Diarrhoea whilst running is a very uncomfort-able feeling, especially on race day. Once you feel that something is not quite right, there is very little you can do to relieve the symptoms other than visit the bathroom. Nervousness on race day can contribute to stomach prob-lems, but by far the commonest cause of 'the trots' is something you ate. Intestinal irritants such as coffee, tea, high concentrations of sugar or food you are intolerant of can be a trigger for unwelcome abdominal discomfort.

Your best chance of avoiding stomach trouble during training and the race is to avoid anything that you know you are sensitive to, especially on race day. Always stick to your usual routine in the hours leading up to the start, and avoid the temptation of sampling any new product that is being promoted to runners. Some runners, in anticipation of a sensitive stomach due to nerves, take an anti-diarrhoea tablet prior to the race to fend off potential problems. Taking medication when not necessary is unadvisable, but if you choose to follow this procedure make sure you have tried it in training. You may inhibit the onset of diarrhoea, but some people can experience stomach cramps as a side-effect of diarrhoea prevention.

CHAPTER 13

Special Precautions for Older and Female Runners

The importance of recognizing our own limitations and unique genetic make-up has been reiterated throughout this book. Whereas for the majority of runners minor training alterations and allowances can be made to suit their individuality, there are some precautions that must be followed among certain groups of people. This should not be interpreted as being patronizing, but rather as respecting the physiological differences between men and women, young and old.

By understanding certain physiological differences, steps can be taken to ensure your training is incident-free and maximum enjoyment can be experienced right up to the finishing line.

THE FEMALE RUNNER

The physical and physiological differences between men and women are obvious in some respects, and less obvious in others. Although most women can train for endurance events without incident, there are a few differences between the female runner and her male counterpart.

Smaller Heart

Women have a distinct disadvantage when compared to men, due to the physical size of their heart and lungs. This makes it very difficult to compete on equal terms. Women's

Running with a grin.

hearts and lungs are generally much smaller in size than men's, which is why their VO2 max levels are lower and exercising heart rate is invariably higher. So if you are training with a male partner and you notice your heart rate is significantly higher than his despite running at the same speed, the likely reason is that you have a smaller heart.

Menstruation and Running

There is no reason why your regular training regime should be impaired by your monthly cycle. As long as normal precautions are taken and uncomfortable symptoms are not severe, running can be maintained at all stages throughout your menstrual cycle. Numerous studies have been carried out to determine the optimum time of the cycle to achieve peak running performance but nearly all of them have been inconclusive. Some studies have suggested that women run better before ovulation, whereas others seem to indicate that performance is enhanced during the flow phase.

As important as this may be to elite athletes, for the majority of women competing in a half or full marathon the issue of comfort is far more important than a slight increase in performance. During your training you will discover for yourself how your monthly cycle affects you, and it is up to you how to manage menstrual discomfort. Women using the contraceptive pill often find that the common symptoms of PMS, such as abdominal discomfort, are alleviated, making running possible at all times of the month. If you are not on the contraceptive pill and suffer badly from PMS, it may be worth visiting your doctor to discuss a short course of a low dose oral contraceptive. You do not have to stay on the medication for long, but for the sake of more comfortable training runs it may be an option worth pursuing. Even if you decide not to use the pill, some women find that their PMS symptoms are in fact alleviated by running, possibly due to the release of endorphins, the body's natural pain-killing hormone.

Whichever way you choose to manage your training with your monthly cycle, there is no need to suffer in silence. If you are experiencing abdominal discomfort and your running is being affected, I strongly advise you to seek medical advice and speak with a friend who may have been helped with a similar problem.

Oligomenorrhea and Amenorrhea

Some female runners experience infrequent or very light periods (oligomenorrhea) and a complete cessation of menstrual flow (amenorrhea). These conditions are usually associated with women who are very light and possess very low levels of body fat, but they can also occur due to frequent high-intensity sessions. The exact reason for these conditions is still not fully understood but alterations to hormone balance are likely to be the cause.

If you find your menstrual cycle is affected by one of these conditions do not be alarmed; normal menstrual function should resume once your training intensity has normalized. If your flow rate remains infrequent or abnormally low after training it is advisable to visit your doctor for a check-up.

Menstrual dysfunction is thought to be caused by:

- low body fat levels;
- low body weight;
- stress;
- poor nutrition and under eating;
- high intensity and frequent training sessions;
- hormonal alterations.

OPPOSITE: Age is no barrier.

Osteoporosis

Also known as 'brittle bone disease', osteoporosis is a degenerative condition where the density of the bones reduces significantly, making them easily broken. More common in women than in men, osteoporosis of varying degrees affects over half of women over fifty, compared to one out of every twelve men. There are a number of reasons why osteoporosis is contracted, but there is overwhelming evidence to support the claim that regular weight-bearing exercise such a running can help significantly in maintainin a high bone density and reduce the chanc of the bones becoming excessively brittle.

The genetic link associated with this diseas means that if there is a known family histor of osteoporosis or easily fractured bone extra care should be taken if you are new t running. Although running can indeed hel improve bone density, excessive exercise ca increase your risk of stress fractures, especiall to the shin bone and the foot.

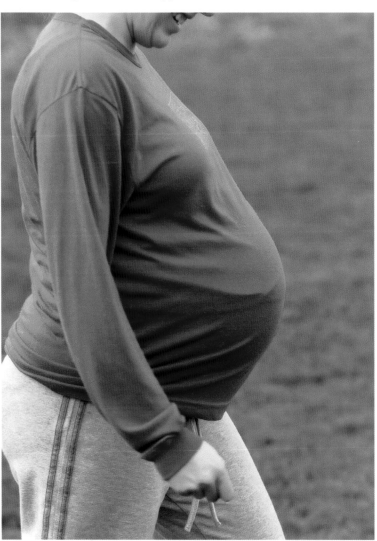

Running during pregnancy should be discussed with your doctor.

Factors that increase your risk of contracting osteoporosis include:

- a family history of the disease;
- amenorrhea or oligomenorrhea;
- smoking;
- poor diet, particularly if is it is low in calcium;
- long periods of inactivity;
- small body frame;
- excessive consumption of alcohol and caffeine.

Pregnancy

Running whilst pregnant is a contentious issue, with many people believing that the two should not mix. This did not, however, stop Sue Olson, an American lady who lined up for a marathon just sixteen days before the birth of her first child. The race went without incident, much to the relief of her husband, who drove parallel to the course in case his first child decide he wanted to enter the world during the race. Running this late in pregnancy is not advisable, but it does highlight that pregnancy need not be an inhibiting factor when it comes to exercise.

The general advice to expectant mothers is that there is no harm in continuing light jogging so long as it is an activity that you are accustomed to. Pregnancy is not a time to suddenly begin running, as your body is simply not used to the stresses that this presents.

Like many controversial issues, common sense should always prevail. Whereas I would not advise any woman to compete in a half or full marathon at any stage during pregnancy, partaking in regular exercise such as light jogging, rowing or cycling can be safe and greatly beneficial to a healthy pregnancy. Advice must be sought from your physician, however.

If you are a seasoned runner and you wish to continue running during your pregnancy

A mature runner finishes the Bristol Half Marathon.

it is important that you first seek advice from your doctor. So long as your practitioner is happy for you to continue light jogging, it is essential that you follow the three basic guidelines for exercising during pregnancy.

Prevention of Hyperthermia
It is best to run in cooler conditions. A warm environment could lead to an increase in internal body temperature, possibly causing heat stress to the foetus.

Prevention of Hypoglycaemia
It is vital that adequate nutrition guidelines are followed to ensure that you have adequate levels of carbohydrate in the body. If your blood sugar levels drop too low it could endanger the availability of glucose to the foetus. Regular sips of a sports drink can help to keep blood sugar levels normal.

Prevention of Hypoxia
The importance of a regular supply of oxygen to the unborn baby is obvious. Concerns have been raised about the effect that exercise can have on the availability of oxygen to the foetus during exercise, so keeping the intensity low is advisable to eliminate the chances of hypoxia.

THE OLDER RUNNER

Age can be a barrier to a number of things in life, but running is certainly not one of them. The number of over-fifties taking part in endurance events has increased immeasurably since the 1980s, proving that the desire and ability to stay fit and healthy into our later years is more prevalent than ever.

All the advice contained in this book is just as applicable to an 18-year-old as it is to an 80-year-old. However, there are just a handful of extra tips for older runners that should be followed to make sure that training goes smoothly and is incident free.

High Blood Pressure

Although not exclusive to older runners, high blood pressure is far more common in older athletes than it is in younger ones. Running with high blood pressure can be extremely dangerous and is not recommended in any circumstances. The lack of obvious symptoms makes high blood pressure especially dangerous, which is why regular check ups are strongly recommended.

Although easy-to-use blood pressure machines now make testing at home very convenient and reasonably accurate, regular trips to your doctor throughout your training is still advised.

Normal blood pressure should read 120/80. If the lower figure regularly shows readings of + or − 10, or the higher figure deviates by + or − 20, a trip to the doctor is strongly advised.

Running Performance

Naturally, as the body ages the ability to perform at the same level as when you were young is diminished. Changes in body composition, VO2 max, strength and cardiac output are all reduced as age gets the better of you, but why should this deter you from training and competing in an endurance race?

Unless you are a very accomplished runner and still strive to be in the top percentage of finishers for your age group, your training should not concentrate on overall speed but instead should maximize the health benefits you are gaining from running regularly. It is not really necessary to incorporate the high-intensity fartlek and interval training sessions, so do not feel your training is inadequate should you choose to leave the fast sessions to the youngsters.

The race itself, whether it is a half or full marathon, should be enjoyed and the old cliché 'It's the taking part that counts' should be in the forefront of your mind.

Running in your later years should not pose any health risks, provided that you know your limitations and your training is not as intense. The tolerance of your heart and muscles is reduced with age, and pushing them to their limits is not advisable. Should you wish to push the boundaries, do so only after a consultation with a professional.

Menopause

Although the male menopause has been highlighted as problematic in some men, the symptoms of the menopause in women are well-documented. There is no reason why the menopause should inhibit your ability to train for the marathon, although special attention must be paid to the increased risk of osteoporosis. During the menopause there is a sharp fall in the production of oestrogen, which contributes to a reduction in bone density. Hormone replacement therapy can help treat common symptoms of the menopause, but this is a very individual decision and one you must take for yourself.

Run, Walk and Cross Train

Running long distances is taxing on a young body, let alone one that has been around for three times longer. You would be asking a lot of your body if you expected to run every step of a marathon, so why place excessive stress on your joints if it is not necessary? During your training, do not feel compelled to follow the training plans in this book religiously. Incorporating periods of walking not only reduces your chances of picking up an injury but helps to make the training runs much more manageable.

How much walking you decide to include in your training sessions is very much up to you, so long as you are gradually adapting your body to tolerate the distance you plan ultimately to run.

Including cross training sessions such as swimming, cycling and rowing are also excellent ways to reduce the stress on the joints and to keep your cardiovascular system in shape. Any exercise which elevates your heart rate is beneficial to your marathon preparations, so as long as you enjoy it, keep doing it.

The time should not matter, it's the finishing that counts.

CHAPTER 14

Race Day

After months of preparation, the day you thought would never arrive eventually does and there is no feeling like it. All the hard work has been done and all that is now left is the small matter of running the race that you have dedicated the past few months of your life to.

On the day of the race you will feel a mixture of emotions, from excitement to anxiety, but it is so important not to forget the procedures that you have practised in training. Every year runners make similar mistakes, which disrupt their race and cause huge disappointment. Poor timing of fluid intake or an excessively rich breakfast in a hotel are all it takes for the beginning of your race to be a very uncomfortable and unpleasant experience.

Although there are countless things out of your control that can go wrong, there are also many things that are well within your control to help ensure that the race starts perfectly.

THE FIRST COUPLE OF HOURS AFTER WAKING

The morning of your first half or full marathon is a time you will always remember. As soon as your alarm sounds on the morning of the race, the butterflies in your stomach begin to fly around as it slowly dawns on you what you are about to attempt.

Nothing can prepare you for how you will feel on the morning of the race, but it is important that you do everything that you have rehearsed in your training and are not tempted to change your routine. Even the smallest of alterations, such as drinking apple juice instead of your usual orange juice, has the potential to cause abdominal discomfort, so stick with what you know.

Breakfast

As soon as you wake up, begin hydrating yourself with small, regular sips of water or sports drink. Try to relax and eat the same breakfast that you have done throughout your training. Whether your breakfast of choice throughout your training has been porridge, toast, muesli or pancakes, stick with it on race day and don't be tempted by a full English breakfast.

Ideally, breakfast should be eaten around 2 to 3 hours before the race to make sure that the food has been digested sufficiently before you run. Eating food too close to the start increases your risk of contracting a stitch.

Leaving the House/Hotel

Before you leave the house or hotel and head for the start line, make sure you have everything that you need. The last thing you need to worry about is forgetting something. Check that you have:

- your race number (with safety pins);
- your foot 'chip' to record your race time (if applicable);
- your heart rate monitor (not essential) or watch;
- waterproofs if necessary;
- plasters on nipples to prevent chafing;

Breakfast – the most important meal of the day.

Waiting for the gun.

Two runners focusing.

- a little money;
- MP3 player;
- race information, including directions to the start line;
- fruit or energy bar;
- water or sports drink – not to be consumed excessively;
- sun cream;
- sun glasses;
- carbo gels or jelly babies.

EN ROUTE TO THE START – MENTAL PREPARATION

Whether you take public transport or are driven to the start line, this is a good time to start mentally preparing yourself for the race. Visualizing yourself in the race is an excellent way to prepare your mind for the challenge ahead.

To help with nerves, try taking deep breaths and force yourself to relax. If you let the anticipation get the better of you, you can end up feeling exhausted before you have even started the race, so use the time travelling to the event to take deep breaths and relax as much as you can.

Remind yourself of what you have already achieved and that you owe it to yourself to put all that you have into the race. You know the going will get tough in the final stages of the race but make a promise to yourself that you won't quit – you will only regret it after the race.

The following are some of the most common techniques that runners use to mentally prepare for the race.

Visualize the Distance

You know how far you have to run, but don't let the distance daunt you. You have done the training and you know that your body is physically prepared for the race; now it's time to prepare your mind. Visualize the race in a number of sections, rather than one long distance. By breaking it up into smaller chunks you will be less intimidated by the thought of running 13.1 or 26.2 miles. By seeing the race as four 3.5 mile runs or four 6 mile runs, it all of a sudden becomes a far less scary prospect.

Visualize How You Will Feel

Whichever distance you are competing in, you know through your training that the final stages are not going to be easy. So why kid yourself? Visualize how your body will feel in the final few miles and make a promise to yourself that you will push through the discomfort. Prepare yourself mentally for how you are going to fight off the overwhelming desire to stop.

You may only ever do this race once in your life. The last thing you want is to feel regret at walking a race you knew you could have run if you had only called upon your mental strength to pull you through.

Breathing Techniques

Deep breathing is an excellent way to calm your mind, body and soul before a big event. Try breathing in for a count of five and out for a count of five. This technique helps to relax you and helps save nervous energy.

Listen to Music

If you have been training with music, listening to the songs that have been blasting into your ears over the past months can help to remind you of what you have gone

Staying hydrated is essential.

through to get to this stage. Whether your music taste is heavy metal or country, try listening to songs that instil emotion in you. Visualizing the race whilst listening to a song that gives you goose bumps can be hugely inspiring and give you the mental focus you need to run a fantastic race.

THE HOUR BEFORE THE GUN

You should aim to be at the start area at least an hour before the gun is fired. This will give you enough time to use the toilet, warm up and stretch.

It is a good idea to drop your belongings off at the designated point in good time so that you can concentrate on preparing yourself for the run, rather than needing to make a last minute dash to catch the lorries that

A runner checking his time chip and trainers.

deliver your bags to the finish. If it is cold make sure you have plenty of old clothes to keep you warm, which you can discard just before the race.

Hydration

At this point, you should be well hydrated. You should have spent the last couple of hours slowly sipping fluids to hydrate yourself adequately. Remember the 'pee test' – if your urine is clear or a light straw coloured then it indicates that you are well hydrated and any fluids you consume after this are surplus to requirements. Needing to go to the loo just minutes into the race is infuriating, so avoid the temptation to take nervous sips of fluid when you are already hydrated.

The Start Line

Keep listening out for the calls to start. It is easy to become immune to the sound of the loud speaker making one announcement after another. The race will not wait for you. Keep an eye on the time and make your way to the start line at least fifteen minutes before the scheduled start time.

Once you line up, the realization of what you have let yourself in for really hits home. The adrenalin will begin to course through your veins and you may very well begin to feel your heart beating away under your vest. Remember to relax and take deep breaths. You know you have done the training and that you are as well prepared as anyone else around you, despite how expensive their running gear looks.

Try to keep moving to avoid your muscles stiffening up. Small jumps and leg movements help to keep you mobilized and encourage blood flow to the legs. Make sure your laces are tied well, your race chip is secure and your trainers feel comfortable.

In the closing minutes as you prepare for a race you will never forget, try to cherish the

The start of any big race is often mayhem.

moment. Focus on how you anticipate running the race, but above all aim to enjoy it.

THE GUN FIRES

Depending on where you are, it can sometimes take a while before you reach the start line. With some races fielding over 40,000 runners, it is not uncommon to take up to 45 minutes before everyone has officially started.

The start of any major race is renowned for being mayhem. With so many legs in such a relatively small area, clashes and falls are common occurrences. As hard as it may be, you must do everything you can to avoid becoming involved in a collision. The start is one of the most likely areas to get injured as a result of tripping over another runner. Try to keep at the side of the road so that you only need worry about what is happening in front of you and on one side. Once the race is well under way space will open up and you will be able to run at your comfortable pace without the fear of tripping up.

Pace Yourself

Settling down into your predetermined running pace can be difficult because of the varying paces of the people running beside you. During the first mile of any major race it is nearly impossible to gauge whether you are running too quickly or too slowly. The combination of adrenalin, a different running

environment and thousands of other competitors running within six inches of you, makes the first mile a bit of a lottery as far as pace setting is concerned.

The golden rule during the first mile of a race is to avoid going off too fast. With so much going on around you, over-pacing the first mile by a minute is easily done. You may feel fine at the time but at the half way stage over-paced miles will catch up on you and the second half of your race will not be pleasant. In my first marathon, I over-paced the first mile by over one minute and at the time I felt absolutely fine. Considering that I ran the first mile at the same pace I completed a fast fartlek interval in, it goes to show the effect that adrenalin has on the body. Needless to say, I found the latter stages of the race more difficult than I should have done.

After mile one, runners gradually begin to spread out more and it becomes easier to settle into your predetermined running pace. The only way to tell accurately if you are on pace is to 'clock' yourself at every mile marker.

RACE TACTICS

How you decide to run the race is a very individual matter. By the time race day comes around you should have a clear idea what you want to achieve – whether it's simply to complete the course without walking, or to finish under a certain time. Whichever it is, you should know how you plan to run the race.

Getting Around the Course

For beginners, or those who have no desire to finish under a certain time, your race tactic should be to run an evenly paced race and avoid the temptation of starting off too fast. The emphasis of the race should be enjoyment. Take time to absorb the atmosphere and reflect on what you have achieved through your training and what you are in the process of achieving.

Remember to follow all of the nutritional advice to ensure you remain well hydrated and you keep your blood sugar levels topped up. Although you may feel that you are not running particularly fast, your body still has to work overtime to keep you moving. If you are overtaken by an oversized vegetable or any other runner in fancy dress, please do not become dispirited – there are some very fast vegetables out there. In my first ever marathon I was overtaken by three oversized tomatoes at the beginning of the race, but had my revenge when I passed them at mile 16.

Timing Your Splits

If you are aiming to finish the race in a specific time, it is essential that you know exactly how quickly you are running each mile. For example, attempting to finish a marathon in under 4 hours without knowing what your mile splits are makes life incredibly difficult.

To finish a marathon in 4 hours, and a half marathon in 2 hours, you need to be running each mile in about 9:09 minutes. By 'running blind' you are unable to tell accurately if you are completing each mile quicker or slower than this. By running faster you run the risk of becoming prematurely fatigued, and by running slower you will have to run faster in the final stages of the race.

To avoid running blind it is a good idea to wear a digital wrist watch with a stopwatch, or a heart rate monitor watch with a stopwatch and 'lap' function. Begin timing as soon as you cross the official start line and check your progress at least every mile.

Conventional Stopwatch

If you are using a stopwatch without a 'lap' function you are going to need to work in

---

OPPOSITE: A runner clocks the time of her mile split.

Two runners enjoying a half marathon.

multiples of 9:09, if we use the example of a 4-hour marathon. Clearly this is not easy to do – mental arithmetic is difficult enough without having to run as well.

To get around this problem, various running websites offer paper wrist bands which you can download and wear whilst running. The bands clearly indicate how much time should have elapsed after each mile in order for you to stay on track for your target finishing time. Alternatively, you can write desired split times on your hand or lower arm.

Watch with 'Lap' Function

By far the easiest option is to use a watch with a lap or split function. This way, every time you complete a mile you simply press a button on the watch and you can see how long has elapsed since you started and how long it has taken/is taking to run each mile. To make life easy for yourself, and for peace of mind that you are on target after every mile, I would strongly recommend that you use this function.

If your goal is to finish the race in a certain time, the pressure is on right from the start. In busy events when the sheer volume of runners means there is very little room to move, the first mile can be very difficult to complete on split. Once you are down on split by sixty seconds it is easy to panic, wondering how you are going to make up the time without exhausting yourself.

Plan Ahead

To give yourself the best chance of achieving your goal, it is important to plan for every eventuality, so that you know how to deal with a situation if it arises during the race. Try the following tactics if you find things are not quite going to plan.

Slow First Mile

Unless you find yourself right at the front of the line-up, it is likely that you will be totally surrounded by people at the start line. In this instance you have to accept the situation and come to terms with the fact that your first mile may very well be slower than it should be.

When you reach the first mile marker, have a look at your split and note how many seconds off it you are. Do not panic. 13.1 and 26.2 miles is a long way and you have plenty of road left to make up for lost time.

Whether you are down by ten seconds or sixty seconds, your focus should be on *gradually* making up the time over the next few miles. There are no rules on how many miles it should take you to grab the time back but you should be thinking along the lines of at least 6 to 10 miles (16km), rather than 1 to 2 miles. By slowly chipping away at the lost time, your body will not be pushed excessively and energy can be preserved.

Fast First Mile

Although it is not an advisable race tactic, adrenalin and excitement can sometimes cause you to significantly over-run the first mile and you can find yourself up to a minute ahead of your split time without any sign of fatigue. If this happens do not be led into believing that you are fitter than you thought or that the buzz of the event will make you run much quicker. If you maintain a pace faster than you have trained for, believe me, it will come back to haunt you later in the race.

If you do find yourself well above pace after mile one, try to relax and consciously ease back a little. This does not mean that you need to slow to a snail's pace, but take your foot off the gas and ease back into a comfortable, relaxing pace. Keep checking how you are doing at each mile marker and make sure you stick close to your predetermined mile splits until the last few miles of the race – then you can go for it.

Positive Splits

Some endurance runners adopt the tactic of 'positive splitting' when it comes to the race. The principle behind positive splits is to purposely run each mile slightly quicker than the split time required to achieve their goal. For example, a marathon runner wishing to complete the race in 3hrs 30mins would need to run each mile in 8:00 minutes to finish in the desired time. If the runner chose to run positive splits, he/she may decide to aim to finish each mile in 7:50 – 7:55 minutes.

By following this tactic, you can gradually knock off seconds after every mile, which will act as a kind of insurance policy in case you encounter problems in the final stages of the race. Some people refer to positive splits as 'putting seconds in the bank'.

The advantage of positive splitting is that as you cover more and more miles you are building up a safeguard so if you are struggling by the end of the race, even if you have banked as few as five seconds every mile, you will find yourself over a minute ahead of schedule. By only running five seconds ahead of split, the body is not being pushed excessively hard and fatiguing early is unlikely.

The disadvantage of positive splitting is that you do run the risk of premature fatigue if your fitness level is on the cusp of being able to achieve your goal. If your training is just adequate to help you achieve your 3:30hrs target (8 minutes/mile), running at 7:55 minutes/mile pace may just be too much to tolerate and you risk fatiguing later in the race. Critics of positive splitting view the tactic as a sure-fire way to actually become fatigued later in the race by running faster than you should.

Sadly there is no way to accurately predict how you will tolerate running positive splits – experience is the only way of finding out. If you are running your first race, it is impossible to know how the race is going to go and how your body tolerates the latter stages of the race. Some runners may benefit from positive splitting; others may begin to tire towards the end.

The best advice is to have a clear idea of how well your training has gone and how confident you feel in being able to achieve your goal. If training has gone so well that you think, for example, 3 hours, 30 minutes is possible, positive splitting may be a tactic to try. Your initial aim of 3 hours, 30 minutes is certainly obtainable and by positive splitting you may even get close to a quicker time.

As always, common sense should prevail. Taking unnecessary risks in your first and maybe last marathon is a risky business.

Negative Splits

The opposite tactic of positive splitting is negative splitting. This is where you purposely run each mile slightly slower for the first half of the race to preserve energy. Every mile in the second half of the race is then performed faster.

If we take the example of a runner with the 3 hours, 30 minutes (8 minutes/mile) target, he/she may run the miles in the first part of the race in an 8:05 minutes/mile split and then target the second half of the race in a pace of 7:55 minutes/mile or quicker.

Provided you have trained effectively for the race, by performing negative splits you should feel very fresh during the second half of the race, helping to inspire you to achieve your goal.

If training has not gone as well as you would have liked and the first half of the race is performed using this tactic, it may be impossible to make up the time in the second half. Some people also find it psychologically difficult to cope with, if they are 'down on

> Irrespective of whether you chose to run the race with positive or negative splits, the most important factor for running a good race is your level of fitness. If you haven't trained hard enough to reach your goal, no tactic can help you run faster.

time' and still have many more miles still left to run.

Experience and individual disposition i once again the key to using this tactic success fully. Some people swear by negative split ting, others believe the tactic is ineffective and pointless.

Whether you choose negative or positive splitting, use your common sense to guide you. Every tactic is used in every running event and they bring as much success as they do failure.

If Things Go Wrong

If you try using any of the above tactics bu don't run as well as you expected, you have to question which factor is to blame. Is it the tactic itself, performing the race tactic incorrectly or the inadequacy of the runner's fitnes through insufficient training? The latter two are the most likely causes of runners failing to achieve their goal.

THE RACE

So you have chosen your tactic, you've overcome the gridlock at the start of the race and you're now in full flow. The way to approach the rest of the race is simple – enjoy it. Stay relaxed, keep a steady pace and soak up the atmosphere of the race of your life.

The sights you will see during the run will keep you amused for miles. Not only will the crowds of well-wishers lining the streets help to keep you smiling, but you fellow runners will also be a source o constant amusement. Whichever event you compete in, there are countless runners who

A runner receives a helping hand to the finish.

hoose to make the race that much harder
or themselves and dress up in a range of
ostumes.

When the Going Gets Tough

Provided that your training has gone according
o plan, there is no reason why the bulk of
he race should be uncomfortable. For at
east three-quarters of the race you should be
unning within your means and remain relaxed
hroughout. It is the final quarter of the race
vhere fatigue and potential low blood sugar
alls upon your mental strength to help you
et through the last few miles.

The marathon is particularly notorious for
nflicting discomfort in runners after mile 18.
This is the point where many people 'hit the

wall' as their glycogen stores begin to run out
and blood sugar levels begin to drop.

It is during the closing stages that your
mental strength and preparation need to be
called upon. The visualization techniques
you performed in the lead up to the race will
help you remember that the discomfort you
are feeling was expected and all the promises
you made to yourself to keep going must be
kept. The famous quote by seven-time Tour
de France winner Lance Armstrong is often
repeated in runner's heads when the going
gets tough:

'Pain is temporary, quitting lasts forever.'

Clearly, when the going gets tough and your
body feels like it has had enough, common

A common sight at the end of any event.

A finisher checks her goody bag.

sense must prevail and you must distinguish between discomfort and illness. If you suffer symptoms of dizziness, disorientation, confusion and nausea it is strongly advised that you stop and seek medical help, no matter how close to the finish you are. Fatigue is one thing; hypotension (low blood pressure), hypoglycaemia and hyponatremia are another.

THE FINISH LINE

The home stretch of any race is an incredible uplifting experience, whatever your running ability. The finish line, for both the serious and charity runner, symbolizes the end of months of hard work and for some people the realization of a lifelong dream – finishing an endurance event. Whilst taking photographs for this book I have had the opportunity to photograph hundreds of runners as they cross the finishing line and the heart-warming sights I have witnessed will stay with me forever.

Whether it is the tired but elated face of an elite athlete crossing the line first, or the tears of joy of a charity runner finishing in memory of a late relative, the finishing line is inspiring for anyone wanting to compete in an endurance event.

AFTER THE RACE

As soon as you have finished the race, you will be ushered through to have your chip removed from your shoe and directed to the area where you collect your bags. Depending on the size of the event, you are usually given a goody bag containing a variety of things such as sports drinks, an energy bar, towels, water bottle, etc.

As much as you will be tempted to crack open a beer to celebrate the end of months of hard training, try to resist and instead spend

OPPOSITE: The moment you've been training for – the finish.

Reebok Bristol
Half Marathon 2006

www.bristolhalfmarathon.com

A cold and exhausted runner hydrates after a race.

the hour after the race re-hydrating yourself. Try to drink at least two litres of fluid in the hour after you have finished, to ensure your hydration status returns to some kind of normality. Only when you have passed the pee test should you really consider having any form of alcoholic beverage.

Once you have retrieved your belongings and been photographed with your finisher's medal, your journey of endurance running has reached its conclusion. However although the race may have finished, the memories of the day will stay with you for the rest of your life.

Inspirational Stories

The increasing popularity of half and full marathons is evident all over the world. Every major event is well over-subscribed and it can sometimes take years to eventually gain a place and compete in your desired event.

By far the most popular form of entry is through charitable organizations for which you must commit to raise a certain amount of money in order to 'pay' for your place. This figure is usually around the £1,500 mark ($2,800), but it does vary from charity to charity.

Although a large proportion of media coverage is given to the elite runners, it is the charity runners who make the marathon what it is. Millions of pounds are raised at every major event for a range of charities all over the world, helping to raise awareness for the plight of others suffering from terminal or incurable diseases.

Every charity runner has a story to tell about the reasons behind their quest to finish a race, which they never imagined possible. The marathon and half marathon inspire people to overcome adversity and help to commemorate the lives of friends and family afflicted with illness.

The following stories were kindly donated by the people telling them, in the hope that their experience will help to inspire others to take up running and raise money for a worthwhile cause.

Mike Charlton at the London Marathon, 2006

At mile 26, with just 400 yards to go of the Flora London Marathon, Nick Martin pulled up with severe cramp that was making running a near-impossibility. Seeing this, fellow runner Mike Charlton stopped and offered a helping hand – wearing a particularly fetching pink tutu.

Within throwing distance of completing his fifth marathon in five weeks in five countries, Mike helped a fellow competitor who was clearly in trouble. Mike said of the incident:

A helping hand.

I must admit that I had absolutely no ideas who he was, he was just another runner in need of a little help. It was the least I could do. The London Marathon is not about times, it's about people. The 50,000 runners with a story to tell, and the millions of spectators willing you to the finish. Therefore I couldn't leave him, it meant more to me to help than it ever would have to sprint to the line.

What made me laugh is the fact that I am ex-military and just reverted to type by screaming in Nick's face to get him to the line... I don't know whether he appreciated it; in fact he actually looked quite scared at the sight of a 6 feet 4 bloke in a tutu shouting obscenities at him.

Felicity and Mark, London Marathon 2006

In the closing stages of the 2006 London Marathon, Mark and Felicity joined hands and crossed the line together in memory of their brother James, who lost his battle against leukaemia on the same day as the 2002 London Marathon. He was just 37.

This is Felicity's account of her motivation for running a distance she never imagined possible.

Mark and I wanted to run the marathon together and chose Children with Leukaemia as our charity, as James loved children (his little girl Seren was only 14 months old when he died).

The support I got from my family during the whole training programme and

Finishing the marathon hand in hand.

on the day of the run itself was incredible. When James was ill we were a remarkably strong family unit – his death devastated us all, but I feel I was able to cope with my grief through the huge depth of love we all felt for him and for each other. That love also kept me going during all the very hard training.

I was also able to focus my thoughts on James while I was running and I found that both comforting and inspiring. I spent a lot of time wondering what he would have thought of his brother and sister (neither of whom had ever shown any inclination towards running before) running 26 miles.

The actual run was hard and very emotional. So many of our family and friends were there to cheer us on at different stages of the run and knowing I would see friendly faces along the route kept me focused. Mark and I were both determined we would run the race together. For me, Mark taking my hand was the most emotional part of the journey. It symbolised our joint love for James as his brother and sister and also our wish to do something 'extraordinary' for ourselves, for other families experiencing leukaemia and mainly for the memory of James who we both miss so very much.

Mike and Helen Painton, Bristol Half Marathon, 2006

After the tragic loss of their daughter to cot death, Mike and Helen Painton decided to commemorate what would have been her 18th birthday by running a half marathon to help raise money for FSID (Foundation for Sudden Infant Death). This is Helen's account of their running challenge.

It was in February 2006 that Mike said he was going to apply for a place in the Bristol half Marathon after I made an off the cuff comment that I would like to run

Finishing makes all the hard training worthwhile.

it to raise money for FSID (Foundation for Sudden Infant Death) as it would be Aimee's 18th birthday in November. I had never run before but Mike had previously run the Bristol Marathon in 1987 and had always wanted to run two more marathons – he had put his medal in with Aimee and wanted to be able to give a medal to our son James and daughter Claire.

We decided to start training together in March. The first time out was horrendous – I couldn't run a mile without stopping, it hurt and I felt fit to drop by the time I got home. I was absolutely convinced that I would not be able to complete the run. I continued to struggle for the next few runs but Mike was ever the optimist, giving me endless support. The first time I was able to run a whole mile it felt amazing, and we celebrated the achievement.

The race itself was incredible and emotional as people were lining the streets clapping and cheering. As we got close to the line, the emotions inside just took over. It was a real mix of pain and pleasure, sadness and ecstasy. The tears just won through in the end.

Stories from Popular Running Events

Every year there are over 800 organized marathons run all over the world, with 384 in the USA alone. The number of half marathons is likely to be far greater. Wherever you live, there will be a number of half and full marathons nearby that you can enter, but most people have their eye on the major events. Almost without question, the two greatest marathons run annually are the London Marathon, usually held towards the end of April, and the New York Marathon held at the beginning of November.

As for half marathons, in the UK by far the most popular is the Great North run held in Gateshead in October, and in America the 'Rock and Roll' half marathon in Virginia regularly attracts 20,000 runners to run the 13.1 mile (21km) course.

Whichever race or event you decide to compete in, big or small, it is vital that you apply for the race as soon as possible, know when the race is run, what the weather is like at that time of the year and most importantly allow plenty of time for your training. You can never have too long to prepare for an endurance event.

If small isn't for you and you have your sights set on one of the big races, the following pages outline some facts about the major half and full marathons in the UK and USA.

The Flora London Marathon

Location: London, England
Capacity: 47,000 runners
Time of year: April
Course profile: Predominantly flat.

Felicity Supple ran the 2006 London Marathon. This is her account:

Although I had been up to London twice before to watch the Marathon and cheer on my husband and cousin's husband, when it came to my actual run I had little idea what to expect. I ran with my brother, so had company the whole time, which was great. However, the atmosphere was so friendly I would have been happy running on my own.

All the runners and supporters met up in Greenwich for the start of the run. It was a truly incredible experience seeing so many thousands of people (men, women, all ages, all sizes) congregating with one thing on their minds. There was a slightly tense atmosphere and people were generally fairly quiet, lost in their thoughts and their mental build-up for the 26 miles ahead.

The start was very exciting. All the runners were herded together and people started to talk more and the camaraderie picked up. With the sheer numbers of runners we walked at first to get to the start line and then started our run.

OPPOSITE: The London Marathon.

I had no real game plan and as a novice marathon runner my goal was simply to finish the 26 miles. I was keen to run all the way but I hadn't set myself a time. My brother and I wanted to stick together so we just tried to settle into a pace that suited us both.

Passing each mile marker was a big psychological boost and the support of the crowds was spine-tingling. Many of the runners were, like us, running for a charity and I kept my eye open for other 'Children with Leukaemia' vests. We had written our names on the front of our vests and having the crowd egging us on by name was a huge help. We had a lot of family and friends also at different landmarks along the way, and knowing we might spot them as we ran kept me going. I was lucky – I saw everyone I was meant to see and was able to shout hello to them all, which was truly fantastic.

New York.

I was very lucky. At no point did I feel I was really struggling and I didn't hit the infamous wall. It was an amazing and enjoyable experience. We had both achieved what we had set out to do. It was one of the best days of my life, and something that has made me feel very proud. Thank you London.

The ING New York City Marathon
Location: New York, USA
Capacity: 35,000 runners
Time of year: November
Course profile: A hilly first mile with slight undulations throughout. Significant inclines can be found at miles 8, 15 and 23 (or 13, 24 and 37km).

Louise Gardiner, 31, from London ran the 2005 New York Marathon for Cystic Fibrosis. This is her account:

My experience of running and taking part in the New York Marathon 2005 is one that I will never forget – the buzz, the excitement, the adrenalin, the euphoria and the agony.

The excitement started with our early morning arrival by bus on Staten Island where, along with 35,000 other runners, I nervously waited for the start as my emotions worked overtime.

As it was my first marathon, the most important thing for me was to enjoy it. Yes, I had a time limit that I wanted to achieve, but I wanted to make sure that I enjoyed every moment. Five bridges, five boroughs and two million spectators lining the course, I was taking in the sights and experiences of one of the world's most vibrant city marathons. And in true American style, the support from the spectators along the way made sure of that. With my name on my t-shirt, I was whooped and cheered along like I was family, to the point that my face hurt so much from smiling. Their support was one of the most important and memorable aspects of the day.

The start of the GNR – the biggest in the UK.

Mile 22 was when I hit my wall but there was no way I was going to stop running at that point. The atmosphere, my fellow runners, and the thrill when I finally entered Central Park kept me going to the long-awaited finishing line.

I absolutely loved it all; the atmosphere was truly amazing and I managed to complete in 4 hours 36 minutes and raise £2,500 ($5,000) for the Cystic Fibrosis charity along the way.

What I learned the most about the marathon was not the actual running of 26.2 miles – that is the easy part – it is the months of training that your mental strength, willpower and need to succeed somehow pulls you through. My training unfolded as a classic drama, carrying doses of comedy, tragedy, joy and pain that all thankfully ended as one of the most memorable and proudest moments of my life.

The BUPA Great North Run
Location: Newcastle, England
Capacity: 55,000 runners
Time of year: October
Course profile: An undulating course with a few steep hills. Due to the number of people, a personal best is unlikely at this event.

Helen Reed, an accountant from Swindon, ran the 2006 Great North Run for Cancer Research. This is her account:

In January 2006, four of us in my office decided to enter for the 2006 Great North Run. To be honest I wasn't that enthusiastic but thought if we all do it together it should be fun and a great way to raise money for my chosen charity, Cancer Research. As (bad) luck would have it, I was the only one who managed to get a place and it dawned on me that I was going to have to face the 13.1 miles on my own. It was my first race and I knew I had months of training in front of me.

The training for the race went well, despite the unavoidable work and social commitments, but I left for the race as well prepared as I could have been.

I travelled up to Newcastle the weekend of the run with a couple of friends from work who had come to support me. The Saturday before the race we got the train into Newcastle to get a feel of the atmosphere of the whole weekend. We watched the children's races and did some sight seeing. It seemed that every other person you talked to was going to be doing the Great North Run.

The next morning was the day of the race and I was up early with nerves. We left the car at South Shields and made our way to the bus that took us to the start. Once we arrived I had to check in my bag and then line up with the other 50,000 people ready to start the race. While I was waiting in the line I got talking to two men who had been doing the race for years and they made me feel at ease.

11.00am, and the race started. By the time I had crossed the start line, the race had been going 19 minutes. The first 2 miles seemed to go really quickly and you could see everyone getting into their pace. I was being overtaken but I was also overtaking people. It didn't seem long before we were running uphill. I wished then that I had done more hill training rather than just the distances.

After 2 hours of running, I remember seeing the welcome sight of the 10 mile mark. At about mile 11 I found myself running next to a couple, and he was nagging her to go faster – which made me so glad I was running on my own at my own pace. A mile before the end I felt I had run out of energy and started to slow down and walk, when a woman running behind me told me not to stop but to keep going, and that we didn't have long to go. So that was it, I really put the last bit of energy I had into it and passed the finishing line in 2 hours 26 minutes.

I really didn't think I would do it again but I have entered again this year and hope to improve on my time.

Further Information

RUNNING GEAR

Adidas Customer Care
PO Box 1512
Chelmsford
Essex
CM1 3YB

Tel: 0870 240 4204
www.adidas.com

Garmin (Europe) Ltd
Liberty House
Hounsdown Business Park
Southampton
Hampshire
SO40 9RB

Tel: 023 8052 4000
www.garmin.com

Nike UK
1 Victory Way
Business Park
Sunderland
SR3 3XF

www.nikerunning.co.uk

Polar Electro (UK) Ltd
Unit L
Heathcote Industrial Estate
Warwick
CV34 6TE

Tel: 01926 310 330
www.polar.fi

Reebok Consumer Advice
Moor Lane Mill
Moor Lane
Lancaster
LA1 1GF

Tel: 0800 30 50 50
www.reebok.com

Ronhill Outdoor & Sports Company Ltd
Redfern House
Dawson Street
Hyde
Cheshire
SK14 1RD

www.ronhill.com

Running Bath
19 High Street
Bath
BA1 5AJ

Tel 01225 462555
www.runningbath.co.uk

ONLINE TRAINING ADVICE AND TIPS

www.marathonconsultancy.co.uk
www.realbuzz.co.uk
www.sweatshop.co.uk
www.runnersworld.co.uk

RUNNING EVENTS

www.bathhalfmarathon.co.uk
www.bristolhalfmarathon.com
www.greatrun.org
www.ingnycmarathon.org
www.london-marathon.co.uk
www.marathonguide.com

FURTHER READING

Colgan, Dr Michael, *Optimum Sports Nutrition* (Advanced Research Press)
Costill, David, and Wilmore, Jack, *Physiology of Sport and Exercise* (Human Kinetics)
Griffin, Jane, *Nutrition for Marathon Running* (Crowood)
O'Connor, Bob et al, *Sports Injuries and Illnesses* (Crowood)

Index

adenosine tri-phosphate (ATP) 32
adrenalin 45
aerobic, anaerobic and VO2 max
    training 37–41
alcohol 128
Allardyce, Barclay 96
Armstrong, Lance 93–4, 161

blood 29
blood pooling 67

caffeine 126–8
capillarization 29, 37
carbohydrates 97, 100–7
charities, running for 165
check-ups 11–12
circulatory system 27, 29
clothing/trainers 17–23
Colgan, Michael 103–4, 106
core stability 59–60
Costilli, David 48
Costilli, William 120
Cracknell, James 36
cross training 71–6
cycling 74–5

dehydration 120, 122–3
Don, Tim 46

electrolytes 125–6
endocrine system 33–4

fats 97–9
female runners 143–8
fluid intake 107, 119–28
fluid loss 120

gadgets for running 24–6
Gebrselassie, Haile 8
glycaemic index 104–6
glycogen 101–5
Great North Run 77–8, 171–2

half marathons 77–84, 169, 171–2
heart 27, 29, 42–52
    cardiovascular drift 51–2
    resting heart rate (RHR) 43–6
heart rate monitors 26, 43
hormones 33–4
    ADH 34
hydration 34, 120
    sports drinks 122–5
    see also fluid intake
hypoglycaemia 102, 105, 107
hyponatremia 125–6

immune system 34–5
injuries 129–42
    Achilles tendonitis 135–7
    acute and superficial 140–2
    anterior compartment syndrome 138
    illio-tibial band syndrome 135
insulin 34
International Olympic Committee 127

lactic acid 38, 50–1, 67
leg muscles 130–1
London Marathon 8, 11, 13, 86, 169–70

marathon training 85–92
medial tibial stress syndrome 138–9
menopause and running 149
menstruation and running 145

minerals 109–18
motivation 93–5
musculoskeletal system/musculature 28,
31–2
    leg muscles 130–1
    muscle fibres 32
music 23

New York Marathon 170–1
nutrition 96–118

older runners 148–9
osteoporosis and running 146–7, 149

piriformis syndrome 139–40
plantar fasciitis 137
posterior compartment syndrome 138–9
pregnancy and running 147–8
prostaglandins 98
proteins 97, 99–100
    amino acids 99

race tactics 157–60
    after the race 162–4
    race 160–2
respiratory system 30–1
R I C E protocol 133, 137
rowing 74
running gait 18–21
    analysis of 19
running intensity 36–41

Salazar, Alberto 41
Scott, Lloyd 8
shin splints 137–8
stretching 53–60
swimming 72, 74

tapering 87
Tergat, Paul 8
therapists/therapy 131–2
trainers/clothing 17–23
training 36–41
    aerobic and anaerobic 37–41
training, importance of variety 61–72
    cross training 71–6
    hill training 69–71
    interval training 66–9
training for half marathon 77–84
treadmills 72
treatments
    ligament tear 133–4
    muscle tear 133

vitamin and mineral supplementation
    107–18
vitamins 97, 107–18

water bottles 23
weight-training programmes 31
Wilmore, Jack 48, 120